Judy Martin's
Ultimate Book of
Quilt Block Patterns

To Barbara,
Best regards,
Judy Martin
Houston 1988

Crosley-Griffith
PUBLISHING COMPANY
Denver, Colorado

This book is dedicated to Shoeless Joe.

ACKNOWLEDGMENTS

Special thanks go to my husband, Steve, for all his help in getting our first self-publishing venture off the ground. Thanks also to my good quilting friends, Marsha McCloskey, and Louise O. Townsend, with whom I have tossed around quilting ideas for years. Thanks to the ladies at my local quilt shops for providing a wealth of fabric from which to choose (and for their friendship, inspiration, and enthusiasm). Thanks to Connie Costo for offering her proofreading expertise. Finally, thanks to my parents for giving me the self-confidence to pursue my dream.

Written and illustrated by Judy Martin
Blocks and quilts made by Judy Martin
Photography by Brian Birlauf, Birlauf and Steen Photography
Typesetting by Janice Bennett, Classic Typography
Separations by American Color Corporation
Printing by American Web

ISBN 0-929589-00-9
Library of Congress Catalog Card Number 88-23700
Published by Crosley-Griffith Publishing Company
3030 Upham Court, Denver, Colorado 80215
First Printing, 1988
15 14 13 12 11 10 9 8 7 6 5 4 3 2 1

Library of Congress Cataloging-in-Publication Data:

Martin, Judy.
    Judy Martin's ultimate book of quilt block patterns.
    Includes index.
    1.Quilting—Patterns. I.Title.
TT835.M379 1988   746.46   88-23700
ISBN 0-929589-00-9

CONTENTS

INDEX OF BLOCK NAMES & ORIGINS

Blocks are listed alphabetically. A source is listed for traditional designs (where known) and for original designs that have appeared in other publications. Of the 174 patterns here, 139 were designed by the author especially for this book. For these, no source is listed. After each name are three numbers; these are page numbers for 1) the color photograph, 2) the block diagram, and 3) the blank drawing for experimentation with color.

INTRODUCTION

Quilt block pattern books have been popular for generations. In 1922, The Ladies' Art Company published *Quilt Pattern Book, Patchwork and Applique.* In 1931, McKim Studios printed *101 Patchwork Patterns.* In 1935, The Caxton Printers, Ltd., released *The Romance of the Patchwork Quilt in America.* More recently, Barbara Brackman's 1979 volume, *An Encyclopedia of Pieced Quilt Patterns* and Jinny Beyer's 1980 book, *The Quilter's Album of Blocks and Borders* stand out. These and other books have documented, illustrated, and made accessible hundreds upon hundreds of quilt blocks. I have used these books and others like them for years. In fact, my favorite quilting books are block books, like these, and books of color photographs, like the *Quilt Engagement Calendars.*

Only recently did it occur to me that none of the quilt block books in my library sported color photos of the blocks. And only *101 Patchwork Patterns* offered full-size patterns for each block. It seemed to me that a new kind of block pattern book was needed: one with color photos and full-size patterns of each and every block. It wasn't long before I found myself immersed in writing this book.

Since I would be sewing each block, I knew I couldn't include every pattern available and still meet the publishing deadline. I decided to limit this book to 174 patterns: only the prettiest, most practical ones. Rather than repeating the most common blocks, I opted to include only a dozen or so classic favorites and another dozen obscure-but-beautiful designs from antique quilts. I selected a few original designs that appeared in black-and-white sketches in my 1983 volume, *Patchworkbook.* For the remaining 139 blocks, I created altogether new (but traditional-looking) designs, ones that have never before been published.

Since I was obviously not setting out to write the FIRST book of quilt block patterns, I thought it was important that I make my book the most beautiful, practical, and thorough— to make mine the ULTIMATE book of quilt block patterns.

Unlike any other block book, this one includes:

1. A coloring book of blank block drawings. The color photos will provide plenty of inspiration and guidance, but you may want to get adventurous and experiment with your own color ideas. You can photocopy the block drawings to color each block as many times as you desire.
2. Full-size patterns for a variety of setting patches. Blocks are, after all, most often made into quilts, and for a quilt you'll need patterns for the sashes or alternate blocks as well as for the blocks.
3. Quilting patterns for the large patches. This adds the perfect finishing touch to your quilt.
4. Seam allowances, grain arrows, and yardages for each patch. The patterns are all accurately drafted and have the points trimmed for easy sewing. Even a beginner should be able to make any of the patterns here.
5. Block ratings for ease of construction. Each rating has a letter designation from A to D to indicate the skill level involved as well as a numerical component to tell you how many patches per square foot the block has, which is a good indication of the time involved.
6. No curves, no set-in patches, nothing tricky or fussy. With so many beautiful, easy-to-make blocks from which to choose, why bother with difficult ones?

THE DELIGHTFUL TRADITION OF BLOCK COLLECTING

Historically, a quilter collected blocks as a means of remembering or saving patterns she might want to make later. These sample blocks were sometimes exchanged among friends. Block collections were also presented as wedding gifts. Some collections were extensive and greatly valued. Occasionally, a woman with an especially fine collection would mention it in her will. One such collection, comprising over 800 blocks, is that of Carrie Hall. These blocks were featured in black-and-white photographs in her 1935 book, *The Romance of the Patchwork Quilt in America.* The collection now belongs to the Spencer Museum of Art at the University of Kansas in Lawrence.

BLOCK COLLECTING TODAY

Nowadays, we have plenty of books documenting block patterns for our reference. However, block collecting is still practical and enjoyable for many reasons. Making one block is a good way to test a pattern for accuracy and to see how you like both the sewing process and the results. It gives you the opportunity to work out fabric and color ideas and to plan which way you want to press seam allowances before you start making your quilt. Making sample blocks is an excellent way for a beginner to learn basic patchwork skills or for a more experienced quilter to master new techniques.

Block collecting is a delightful hobby, and a very inexpensive one. Some people collect postcards or stamps; others prefer antiques, dolls, china plates, or thimbles. Why not quilt blocks? If you already collect fabric or quilts, blocks are the logical next step. Blocks take very little space, and you can display them on the wall, with or without picture frames. You can stitch them into small projects such as photo album covers or toss pillows. You can join them into sampler quilts. Or you can simply enjoy them for their own special charm.

These days, it seems that no one has time for big projects. If you have enough to do juggling a home and a career, you may enjoy the near-instant gratification of making quilt blocks in whatever spare time you can muster. Do you have more ideas than you'll ever get around to making into quilts? Do you lack space to store or money to buy supplies for all the quilts you'd like to make? Do you want to make meaningful, handmade gifts that are not as time-consuming or expensive as full-size quilts? Would you like to keep a memento of every quilt you have made and parted with or every fabric you have used? Are you fascinated with the tremendous variety of quilt blocks? Would you like to share a fun and interesting hobby with other quilters from around the world? If so, you will surely enjoy quilt block collecting.

MAKING QUILT BLOCKS IN THE NAME OF FRIENDSHIP

Block Exchanges. Many quilters enjoy making contact with other quilters around the world by exchanging blocks. You can place a notice in one of several quilting magazines, or you can start by contacting others who have done so. Most quilters specify a block size; some also indicate a theme or color preference. Exchanging quilt blocks can be a fun way to make friends with others sharing the same interests.

If you have a number of quilting friends, you may want to form a group to swap blocks for very special friendship quilts. Each member requests blocks conforming to her chosen theme. She might choose scraps, blocks with flower names, a blue-and-rust color scheme, or whatever. Set a reasonable deadline by which time each member will have made and received a block from every other member.

If you are building a block collection and you also enjoy block exchanging, here's a timesaving idea: When you make a block for your collection, make a second one just like it to swap. Cutting and stitching two blocks at a time makes more efficient use of your time and materials, and it lets you keep a memento of what you sent in the exchange.

Make a number of identical blocks to swap with friends and acquaintances, if you like. You can use all of your speediest techniques, just as you would if you were making an entire quilt. This block can be your signature block, the one you are known by.

Friendship Quilts. Another wonderful use for quilt blocks is the making of presentation quilts and album samplers. Since the early 1800s, these quilts have been made by groups of people to honor their special friends and loved ones. Nowadays, these quilts are called friendship quilts. Each person makes one block; then the blocks are joined to form a quilt, which may be quilted by the whole group or by an individual. Blocks may be different patterns (as in a sampler quilt), or the same pattern may be made up in different fabrics. Often, each maker signs her own block.

Quilt guilds, church groups, and families often make group friendship quilts of this type today. The quilt may be intended as a wedding gift, a retirement memento, or a 50th anniversary present. Sometimes, the quilts are made for a fund-raising auction or raffle or for a charity such as a homeless shelter, a children's hospital or hospice, a safe-house for battered women, or a nursing home.

I can think of no more loving gift than a quilt made by many willing hands, so I am a great proponent of friendship quilts. My most cherished possession is a friendship quilt made by my coworkers on the occasion of my wedding. Men and women—quilters and people who had never picked up a needle—participated in the joint effort. The quilt is a beauty, but even if it had been ungainly, I would prize it just as much.

Should you find yourself in the position of coordinating or participating in a friendship quilt project, you will find this book most helpful. Each participant having a copy of the book can choose his or her favorite pattern. Specify a block size. These are all 10″, 12″, or 14″, the most popular sizes. Hold a workshop to teach the basics to any beginners in the group. If participants are far afield, the beginners among them will appreciate the book's quiltmaking instructions. They will also find that the color photos provide inspiration and guidance for their first attempts at combining fabrics for a quilt block. Allow ample time for the slowest of quilters to finish their blocks, but do set a deadline. Enjoy the spirit of camaraderie that these projects bring out, and rest assured that you will be making your lucky recipient feel very loved.

Block exchanges and friendship quilts are great for spreading goodwill and sharing all the warmth and caring

that everyone knows is stitched into a patchwork gift.

EVERY BLOCK A QUILT PATTERN

Of course, the primary use for quilt blocks is for making patchwork quilts. Any block shown can be made into a quilt. The block is the primary unit of design and construction needed for a quilt. Simply make a number of blocks, either identical or in different colors or fabrics—even different patterns—and join them in rows to make a quilt.

The section on quilt planning discusses a number of ways to arrange blocks to form a quilt. The six basic arrangements are illustrated in the larger color photographs scattered among the block photos.

YOUR FAMILY HISTORY PRESERVED IN A QUILT: THE PERSONAL HISTORY SAMPLER QUILT

Blocks traditionally have been named for people, places, and things that are singled out for being familiar and comfortable or exotic and memorable. Grandma's Favorite, Weathervane, Martha Washington Star, Skyrocket, and Mexican Star are a few old examples. The new blocks in this book also have been named in this tradition. You will find regional place names, hometowns, vacation destinations, and other places from your past. There are blocks named for sisters, brothers, mothers, fathers, and other family members. Block names denote a variety of trades and occupations as well as hobbies and special interests, birthstones, months and days of the week, personal attributes, and more.

Quilters seem to take special joy in selecting blocks not only for their aesthetic qualities, but also for their names. The blocks can paint a pretty picture and tell a story, as well. Your quilt can be a personal history or a family sampler. You can select blocks whose names have special meaning for you or for the person for whom you are making the quilt. Blocks can represent places you have visited, what you do for a living, what you do for fun, people in your life, and so on. Many of the blocks can be used for several purposes. For example, Hollywood Star might be chosen for a star performer or for one who lives in or has enjoyed a visit to Hollywood; Viennese Waltz might commemorate a trip to Vienna or it might suggest an interest in ballroom dancing. Scan the index on page 6 to see the possibilities for your own personal history sampler quilt.

By way of example, I have made my own personal history sampler quilt, which is shown on the inside front cover. Blocks are ones whose names are meaningful to me. I used blocks in a variety of sizes, adding plain or pieced strips where necessary to join the blocks in rows or other manageable units.

A PERSONAL INVITATION

I so thoroughly enjoyed working on this book and I have so many more ideas on the subject of blocks that I have already started working on a second volume of *Judy Martin's Ultimate Book of Quilt Block Patterns.* (More about it is on page 99.) I'd love to include pictures of YOUR personal history sampler or YOUR own original block patterns. If you would like to share your handiwork in Volume 2, please send a photograph along with a self-addressed, stamped envelope, and we'll gladly consider it.

QUICK QUILTMAKING METHODS

In this section, I present the methods that I use in quiltmaking. My approach to cutting and piecing is based on standard dressmaking procedures, and it calls for no special skills or equipment that you wouldn't already have for any other kind of sewing project. If you are a sewing enthusiast who has never before made a quilt, you will find this method natural and easy to learn. If you are an experienced quilter, you will find some helpful information in this section, as well. Even if you have your own methods, you can benefit from the suggestions for choosing fabrics, pressing, perfecting joints, and so forth.

CHOOSING COLORS & FABRICS

Your choice of colors and fabrics can make a profound difference on the character of your finished block or quilt. A simple Pinwheel block looks riotous made from a red bandanna print combined with a bright blue calico and a crisp white print with red firetrucks and blue policemen. The same Pinwheel looks serene in the monochromatic blue combination shown on page 30.

For many of you, choosing colors and fabrics is the most enjoyable step in making a quilt. It is here that you get to exercise your creativity, to add your own personal touches to a pattern. For others of you, perhaps, choosing fabrics seems like a guessing game, one for which you haven't a clue. Of course, when you know how to play the game, you will have a lot more fun. With practice, you may get to be very good at it, too.

Since it takes so much less time to make a block than it takes to make a whole quilt, those of you who like choosing fabrics get to do it much more often as a block collector. And those who are intimidated by the prospect of choosing fabrics benefit as well. Not much time or fabric is wasted when your block is less than perfect. Often it is easy to see what you have done wrong, and better yet, you can fix it quickly and easily. Perhaps all it needs is a little more contrast here or a brighter accent there. Making blocks will give you valuable practice in choosing colors and fabrics. And with practice come skill and confidence. Once you start to have success with your color choices, you will doubtless start to enjoy this step in the quiltmaking process.

How do you get started learning the color game? What are the ground rules? Let's start with the object of the game. It is not to choose the "right" colors. It is not to choose the color combination that most people like. The object is to choose a color scheme that *you* like. That shouldn't be too hard, should it?

You can start by looking at the color photos of blocks in this book. Make a list of blocks whose color schemes and fabrics appeal to you. Now look at the blocks on your list again. What do they have in common? Did you choose only the blue blocks? Or the purple ones? Did you choose monochromatic blocks? Multicolored ones? Blocks with many fabrics? Or few fabrics? Blocks with soft colors? Blocks that "glow"? Blocks that gradate? Bright blocks? Blocks with busy prints? Blocks with prints positioned carefully for special effects? Once you start to verbalize what you like and don't like, it becomes easier to choose fabric combinations that are going to please you when you start making blocks.

If you find a block with a color scheme that you like, you can make a block just like it. Or, if you like the colors of one block and the pattern of another, you can rework the pattern in your chosen colors.

My favorite way to come up with a winning color scheme is to start with a favorite multicolored print. I then add fabrics to match the accent colors in the print. For example, I might start with a blue print with pink roses and green leaves. I'll add prints in one or two shades of pink and a floral stripe in white with pink and green accents.

I keep a stash of fabric on hand so that when I'm gearing up to make a block or quilt, I can just start pulling fabric off my shelves. I find that buying three-quarters of a yard to one-and-one-half yards of each fabric is sufficient for most of my projects, although I may buy more if I think the fabric would make an especially lovely border or alternate block.

I pull down more fabrics than I need for the project at hand. In fact, I pull down anything remotely close to my intended theme. I start stacking and staggering the folded fabrics, eliminating those that detract from the mix. Sometimes, I'll pass the collected fabrics in front of my stash to find a suitable accent. I try to vary the look of the prints, including prints of various sizes and characters.

Sometimes, I start with a block and then choose the colors and fabrics; at other times I start with the fabrics. Sometimes I color a block drawing, and sometimes I simply start cutting patches from fabric.

Occasionally, I'll cut a large print, floral stripe, or widely spaced motif with patches carefully centered over a particular part of the print to achieve a special effect. This adds a formal, elegant touch to a block. At other times, I'll cut patches from different parts of a large print for a casual look with an added spark of interest.

Please don't be intimidated by choosing fabrics. It is simply a matter of learning to recognize what you like when you see it. If you keep your mind open and you aren't afraid of looking foolish, you'll be in the best possible situation for learning about color. As you pull fabrics from your stash, you'll feel free to try all sorts of outlandish combinations. Some will be awful, which is pretty much what you expected, but others will be wonderfully refreshing and delightful. You'll never grow unless you try.

Having just told you that the object of the game is to please yourself, I might appear a little foolish if I tried to establish hard-and-fast rules. You may not like the same things that I do. However, I find that verbalizing what has worked for me in the past helps me to make successful blocks time after time. Therefore, I offer for your consideration some guidelines that I follow. Feel free to adapt them to suit yourself.

1. Experiment with color combinations for your block by coloring a block drawing with felt pens, crayons, or colored pencils. If you think you'll want to try more than one coloring, photocopy the block drawing and color the copies.

2. Aim for variety in value, scale, and visual texture. That is, include light, medium, and dark shades; small, medium, and large prints; and printed figures of many different characters: dotty, striped, fluid, regimented, organic, geometric, sparse, busy, sketchy, detailed, and so on.

3. Study your fabrics together before you start to make the block. Arrange and rearrange them to see which ones look best next to each other. Do they blend or contrast in the right places for the pattern that you have in mind? Do they appear too busy or boring together?

4. If you will be using a linear pattern, such as a stripe, is there a balanced way of using it in your pattern?

5. Cut out the block and arrange the pieces on a table or flannel board. Study the effect. Live with it for a few hours or a few days while you work on something else. A finished block always looks better than the patches on the table. Still, if you dislike the block now, you probably won't like it after you sew the patches together. Decide whether any changes would improve the block, and cut out any replacement

pieces to judge their effect. By the time you are ready to sew the block, you should have ironed out any possible problems.

6. After you make the block, look at it critically. What do you especially like about it? Even if you like the block, is there something you could improve upon next time? Treat each block as a learning opportunity. You may start out learning from your mistakes, but before long, you'll be learning from your successes, as well.

PLANNING YOUR QUILT

You won't need to worry much about quilt planning and yardage if you are simply making blocks for your collection. However, if you want to make a quilt from any of these block patterns, you will want to plan how to arrange

your blocks for a quilt and determine how much fabric to buy.

Arranging Blocks in the Six Basic Sets. Start by deciding on a set, that is, an arrangement for your blocks. The basic sets are illustrated in color photographs on pages 20, 23, 25, 27, 30, and 32.

For the most obvious of sets, blocks are joined side by side in straight rows. For another setting possibility, blocks can be separated by strips called sashes. Small, square patches called setting squares are placed at the intersections of lengthwise and crosswise sashes. Another arrangement calls for alternate plain blocks. These are plain squares the same size as the blocks. These plain squares are sewn between blocks in a checkerboard pattern.

With or without sashes or alternate plain squares, blocks can be sewn together in straight rows across and down the quilt, or they can be tilted so that the blocks' corners are at the top. The tilted arrangement is called a diagonal set. Here, the rows run from corner to corner of the quilt rather than from side to side.

By combining straight or diagonal arrangements with blocks set side by side, with sashes, or with alternate plain blocks, we come up with six basic sets. They are:
1. Blocks set side by side in straight rows.
2. Blocks set side by side in diagonal rows.
3. Blocks set with sashes in straight rows.
4. Blocks set with sashes in diagonal rows.
5. Blocks set with alternate plain squares in straight rows.
6. Blocks set with alternate plain squares in diagonal rows.

The best blocks for side-by-side sets are those that form secondary patterns where the blocks touch. Sometimes, a block will surprise you with a lovely secondary pattern. A good way to anticipate this is to trace or photocopy the block drawing several times and put the copies side by side. Do you see a new pattern emerging where four blocks meet? Good examples of blocks that form secondary patterns when they are set side by side include Teacher's Pet, page 34; Diamond Jubilee, page 19; and Bonny Scotland, page 19. If you prefer a more direct approach, you can simply make a number of blocks and spread them out side by side to judge the effect.

Good candidates for sashes and alternate blocks are patterns that have a lot of points around the edges. A few examples are Patience Patchwork, page 33; Roll On, Columbia, page 24; and February's Finest, page 34. These can be tricky to sew to neighboring blocks, but the sewing is greatly simplified if the blocks have sashing strips or plain blocks separating them. Narrow sashing strips can be quite unobtrusive, and secondary patterns will be scarcely interrupted by them. Wider sashes serve to segregate the blocks more fully. Alternate plain blocks isolate the blocks most of all. The piecing is minimized in an alternate block arrangement because you will need to make only half as many blocks, but you will surely want to lavish more quilting on a quilt of this style.

Designing Your Personal History Sampler. You can make a quilt telling your own story or the story of the person for whom you are making the quilt. If you like, modify the idea to make a *family* history quilt, with blocks representing each family member and his or her interests. The personal history sampler on the inside cover is also a good model for assembling blocks from your collection or those that you have received in block exchanges. If you have made and parted with many quilts, you might like to make a sampler that includes blocks representing each of the quilts that you have made. Finally, if you are a fabric collector, you might enjoy making this kind of sampler as a keepsake of favorite fabrics in your collection. If you acquire fabric in the course of your travels, you could choose blocks whose names suggest the places where you purchased the fabrics.

After you have decided on a theme for your sampler quilt, look over the index on page 6 and list appropriate block names. If you like, you can model your quilt after the one I made, substituting appropriate blocks. You can pare your list down to the same number of blocks of each size as I have used in the quilt in the photo. In this case, use the quilt plan on page 55. If you want a larger quilt, you can repeat a row or two. (If you turn the repeated row with the opposite edge up and select different blocks, it won't look like a repeat at all.) If you want a smaller quilt, you can delete some blocks around the edges and square off any odd spaces with filler patches.

If you are feeling adventurous, you can plan an altogether different arrangement of blocks. You can simply make blocks and then plan the arrangement and fillers, or you can map it all out on graph paper in advance. Even if you have made the blocks without benefit of a plan, you will want a scale drawing of the quilt when it comes time to make the fillers and join the blocks. Draw the quilt to scale on graph paper with one graph square representing one inch in the quilt. It is not necessary to draw each block in detail. You can simply indicate a ten-, twelve-, or fourteen-inch square. You can work out the details of the remaining spaces, utilizing basic patterns from the book, such as one- and two-inch squares and two-inch right triangles. Do try to keep the construction simple by relying on rows or other straightforward units.

If you prefer a less random look, you can simply frame each ten-inch block with four two-inch strips and frame each twelve-inch block with four one-inch strips. This way, each block ends up fourteen inches. You can join the blocks with sashes, alternate blocks, or side by side in the traditional set of your choice.

Determining Yardage. The charts on pages 66-67 will help you juggle your chosen set and your desired quilt size to come up with a workable quilt plan. That in hand, you'll need to count blocks and determine how many patches of each shape, size, and color are needed to make your quilt. You will find that the formulas on page 68 are helpful for this. Once you've figured these requirements, you can find the proper yardage for each patch and fabric in the chart on page 66.

CUTTING THE FAST, ACCURATE WAY

I'm a self-taught quilter who made quilts for over ten years before learning how most people do it. I was astonished to find out later that people marked and cut patches one at a time. It never occurred to me to do it that way. My experience had been in dressmaking. I was accustomed to pinning a paper pattern to doubled fabric when I cut. When I stitched, I guided the edge of the fabric along a seam gauge on the throat plate of the sewing machine. That's how I made my clothes, and that's how I did my patchwork, also. I probably would not be a quiltmaker today if I'd had to make that first quilt using time-consuming traditional methods. I'm not that patient. You may enjoy handwork. If so, I respect

that. Please feel free to continue to make quilts your own way. However, if you've been longing for a shortcut and you are comfortable with a sewing machine, read on.

If you've ever used a sewing machine to make a simple skirt or dress, you'll find this method to be quite natural. The method is quick, accurate, and versatile, as well.

Forget about templates. Instead, you will be using paper patterns (as you do in dressmaking). The paper need not be heavy. In fact, it should be flexible. Sturdy, deluxe tracing paper or graph paper are ideal. Trace or rule your pattern with seam allowances included. (There's no need to trace the seam lines. The cutting lines will suffice.) Fold your fabric, with selvedges together, on your ironing board. Press. Fold again to make four layers, if desired. Press again. The layers should be smooth and even. Pin your pattern to the top layer, observing grain lines. (If you pin through all four layers, the pattern will bow down around the pin and flip up around the edges. It is easier to cut accurately with the pin only catching the top layer.) Cut around the pattern through all layers with good, sharp scissors. Be careful not to shift the layers of fabric as you cut. Hold the scissors straight, not angled, so that the blades cut through all layers with a vertical stroke. If your scissors are angled, patches on the bottom layer may be larger or smaller than ones on the top layer. Use somewhat short strokes, cutting in the middle of the blades rather than at the tip or back. (Cutting at the tip makes for little, mincing strokes that are jerky and inefficient. Cutting at the back of the blade lifts the fabric too much and makes it difficult to keep the layers even and the pattern in place.)

Be sure to cut off the points of the patches as indicated on the patterns. This will provide clues for positioning patches for machine piecing, and it will reduce bulk in the seam allowances. Cut patches edge to edge, aligning the pattern piece with the edge already cut for the last patch. You don't need to trim off the selvedge, but avoid it when you position your pattern for cutting. The selvedge may shrink disproportionately, causing billows, or it may be printed with the manufacturer's name or have perforations or an unprinted edge that will look like a glaring error if it shows up in your quilt. It is best to simply steer clear of the selvedge. If your pattern gets dog-eared, make a new one. Cut the largest patches first; smaller patches can be cut from the leftovers.

If you are cutting symmetrical patches, such as squares, diamonds, rectangles, isosceles triangles (having two sides the same length), kites, octagons, arrows, or trapezoids, you can turn the pattern over after you cut each stack of four. The pattern will curl up as you cut, and by turning it over, you can flatten it again.

Occasionally, a pattern calls for asymmetrical patches (ones that are different when viewed from the back). Rhombuses (G patches on pages 84-86), parallelograms (E1-E3), and many of the more unusual triangles (such as C1-C5) are asymmetrical. If you need to cut mirror images of these in equal numbers, you can follow the usual layer-cutting procedure. If you need to cut asymmetrical patches without their reverses, you'll have to unfold the fabric. Cut

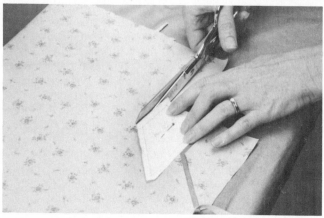

one patch at a time, being careful to keep the patch right side up as you cut each patch. If you need to cut the same asymmetrical shape from several fabrics, you can layer the different materials, keeping each right side up.

That's all there is to cutting. No marking is needed. In fact, as you gain experience, you will find that you can simply hold the pattern in place with your fingers without pinning. As you cut, move your fingers as needed to keep the pattern in place. If the pattern gets jostled, simply reposition it.

GETTING READY FOR PIECING

A piecing diagram is included for each block in the book to show you the piecing sequence. Still, you'll probably find it helpful to lay out your patches in their proper positions and pick them up as you prepare to stitch them together. I've been making patchwork quilts for almost twenty years, and I still lay out the patches for a block in this way. If I haven't done so, I'll invariably make mistakes.

In general, you will be sewing patches together to make rows or other units, which are then joined to complete the block. Go back to the patches that you have laid out on the table. Spread the patches apart between units or rows, referring to the piecing diagram.

SETTING UP A PERFECT SEAM GAUGE FOR YOUR SEWING MACHINE

There are three keys to precision patchwork. The first is an accurate pattern. No problem. Simply take any pattern

straight from the book. The second key is accurate cutting. Simply cut your fabric patches to exactly match the patterns. The final key is accurate sewing, which boils down to following an accurate seam gauge. This is where most quilters who have problems get into trouble.

Once I took my sewing machine to a friend's house to help her make Log Cabin drink coasters for a crafts fair. She had already cut out the strips. We set up our sewing machines at opposite ends of the kitchen table and started working. We got involved in conversation, and an hour had passed before we knew it. More conversation, more time, more little Log Cabins. At some point in the proceedings, one of us stopped working long enough to survey the growing pile of coasters. We seemed to have a problem: My blocks were a half inch larger than hers! How could that be? Different ideas of a ¼" seam allowance, it seems. I was using a tape marker and she was using the edge of her presser foot as a guide. The difference in our seam gauges was only slight, but the difference in the completed blocks was quite noticeable. We were lucky. Log Cabin blocks are pretty forgiving, and we were able to make use of all of the coasters (in sets of two sizes), after all. We realized, though, that had we been making some other pattern, we could have had a mess on our hands. The problems arise when one part of the block has more seam allowances than another part. If your seam allowances are imprecise, then the various parts of the block will not fit together.

Check your seam gauge right now. You may be surprised to find that your seam allowances are not exactly ¼" deep, especially if you have been using the edge of your presser foot as a guide. Here are two ways of correcting the problem:

If you like to use the edge of your presser foot as a guide, you may want to make your seam allowances match that measurement even if it is not exactly ¼". To do this, trace or draft your pattern piece without seam allowances, leaving some space all around. Do not cut it out. Insert this pattern to the *right* of your sewing machine's needle with the seam line along the right edge of the presser foot and the needle outside of the patch. Stitch without thread, following the seam line with the edge of the presser foot. Cut along the perforations made by the needle. Add this special seam allowance to every pattern piece.

If you prefer exact ¼" seam allowances, as given on the patterns in this book, you have a couple of options. If you have a zig-zag machine, you may be able to adjust your needle position to make perfect ¼" seams using the presser foot as a guide. Simply trace a pattern from the book, including seam lines as well as cutting lines. Align the edge of the presser foot with the cutting line of the pattern. Adjust the needle until it aligns perfectly with the seam line.

If you can't adjust your needle, you can insert the pattern under the needle, lower the presser foot, and stitch on the seam line for several inches to make sure it is feeding straight. With the paper pattern still in place and the presser foot still down, put a piece of masking tape on the throat plate of the machine right along the cutting line of the pattern. Use the edge of the tape, rather than your presser foot, as a seam gauge.

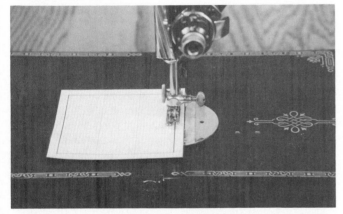

PIECING THE EASIEST, MOST EFFICIENT WAY

Years ago, when both of us were still fledgling quilters, Marsha McCloskey and I got together to share techniques and ideas. (We still do.) I showed her how I drafted paper patterns and cut them out without marking. She suggested an improvement: cutting out on the ironing board. (This was a real back saver after I'd been cutting out on the floor. Now, fifteen years later, my back and I are even more grateful to Marsha for the tip.) I introduced Marsha to a seam ripper (we all make mistakes from time to time). And I showed her how to cut off points to align the patches properly for piecing.

It was Marsha who told me about chain piecing. She described sewing one pair of patches together and then, without stopping to lift the presser foot, continuing right on stitching the next pair of patches. She said that her young daughter, Amanda, would ready the pairs of patches and hand them to her. Marsha raved about the method, but I'm afraid I resisted chain piecing awhile because I didn't have anyone to help me get the next pair of patches ready. I'm embarrassed to say that it didn't occur to me that I could lift my foot off the pedal and pause to get the next pair of patches ready to sew myself.

Once I tried chain piecing, I was hooked. You can sew as fast or as slowly as you like. The great advantage is that you avoid all those nasty thread ends and snarly knots that come with starting and stopping the usual way. You can save a great deal of thread (and bobbin winding), and you can avoid the tedious snipping of threads on the back of your quilt, a chore that delays your enjoyment upon completing your quilt top.

Chain Piecing Method. Here is the method: Join two patches in a seam, stitching from edge to edge of the patches and backtacking at both ends. Come to a stop, but leave the presser foot down. Prepare the next pair of patches. Slip the next pair of patches under the tip of the presser foot (without lifting it). Stitch through thin air for a couple of stitches until the second pair of patches reaches the needle.

Stitch the second pair of patches together, backtacking at both ends. The first pair of patches will be attached by a twist of thread. Continue joining patches in pairs. Snip the threads between pairs when you are ready to go on to the next step.

Some machines balk at stitching right up to the edge of the fabric. They may push the fabric down the hole or make a huge knot on the bobbin side. This is not such a problem when you are chain piecing. With no long thread tails to tangle, the stitching proceeds more smoothly. I've found that it is also helpful to avoid stitching over the edge of the fabric in reverse. I make it a point to start and end each seam on a forward stitch. I stop about one stitch shy of the edge when I backtack, and I never have problems with snarls and tangles. For the same reason, I also make it a point to stitch from the square end of a triangle toward the pointed end wherever possible. Occasionally, the pointed end can get pushed down the hole with the needle if you start your line of stitching there.

Assembly-Line Method. Assembly-line strategies go hand-in-hand with chain piecing. With this approach, you sew all of the A patches to all of the B patches for the entire quilt. Then you add a C patch to each pair, and so on until you have completed all of the blocks. This can be tedious, and it can be dangerous. You can repeat a mistake hundreds of times before you know it. I modify the asssembly-line idea to make it more interesting and to allow me to use the approach to piece a single block. Most blocks have four corners alike, so I repeat each step four times. I simply snip the chains apart as I complete the fourth repeat of each step. It is not until the final step that I have to lift the presser foot and break the chain.

For example, to make the Judy's Star block (diagram on page 36), I start by joining an A7 square to a B10 triangle. I repeat this step to make four of these units. I leave the last unit under the presser foot and snip apart the other three. Then I add a B17 to each of the three units. By this time, the fourth unit is clear of the presser foot, and I snip it off and attach a B17 to it. The idea is to repeat each step for the matching parts of the block without ever lifting the presser foot. The description gets a little tedious, but if you care to follow along, referring to the diagram, you can see how this works for the whole block. The next step is to snip off the other three A7-B10-B17 units, now that they are clear of the presser foot. Next I sew one of these units to the A11 square. To two more of the A7-B10-B17 units I sew another B17. Now I can snip off the fourth of these A7-B10-B17 units as well as the unit with the large A11 square. I sew these together. I snip off the other two A7-B10-B17-B17 units and add another B17 to each. I can now snip off the A11 unit and the first of the other two units. I join them. Finally, I lift the presser foot and cut the threads before taking the final seam to complete the block.

Another way to adapt assembly-line strategies is to make two identical blocks at a time. Repeat every step for the second block, and you won't have to break the chain by lifting the presser foot at all. This works well for entire quilts, and it works well for block collectors who like to make one block to keep and a second one to exchange.

Additional Machine Stitching Pointers. Beginners often ask me about needles, thread, and pinning. Here are a few suggestions to get you started. Make sure your sewing machine is outfitted with a number eleven (broadcloth) needle. Anything lighter may be too fragile. Anything heavier may make unnecessarily large holes. Change the needle at the first sign of a burr. Needles are inexpensive, and a burred one can run your fabric and spoil your quilt.

Choose a neutral thread color. I usually use beige. It is not necessary to change thread to match the fabric for every seam. If you are concerned about the stitches showing, match the thread to the fabric toward which you will be pressing the seam allowances. If you have a number of bobbins wound ahead of time, some with dark thread and others with light, it is a simple matter to pop in a different bobbin when you're going to be stitching on a border or sewing a whole slew of assembly-line patches the same color. You can leave your beige thread on the top and stitch patches with a dark bobbin and the dark patch down. Wind plenty of bobbins. A single bobbin will make about eight blocks.

Ten stitches per inch makes a perfect seam. A shorter stitch makes an unnaturally firm seam that is difficult to rip out in case of error. A longer stitch makes a seam that is neither firm nor sturdy.

Pin long seams at intervals of about four inches. Pin at each joint to be matched, and pin borders at ends, centers, then at intervals of about four to six inches. It is not necessary to pin seams shorter than about fifteen inches when no matching is needed.

If your cutting and sewing are accurate, there should be no need to fudge. However, if you should ever need to ease one side of a seam, stitch it with the full side down. The machine will take up the slack for you.

When you place patches face to face in position for stitching, align their raw edges and ends. The points of the pattern pieces in this book have been pretrimmed at the proper angle to align with neighboring patches. You don't have to guess how far a point should extend, and you don't have to mark seam lines in order to align the patches properly for seaming.

Be consistent when joining patches assembly-line style. Always stitch patches with the same lead edge and the same patch on top. This way, you'll avoid careless mistakes.

PERFECTING YOUR POINTS & JOINTS

Generally, in patchwork, seam allowances are pressed to one side rather than being pressed open. This keeps the batting from seeping through the spaces between the stitches. It also forms ridges that will help you align seams perfectly at joints. Here's how:

When you are preparing to stitch across a joint, press the seam allowances in opposite directions. Hold the joint

between your thumb and forefinger and slide the two halves until they stop at the ridge formed by the seam allowances. At this point, the joint matches perfectly. Stick a pin in at an

angle across both sets of seam allowances, and stitch. Wherever possible, turn the unit so that you are stitching across the seam allowance on the top side before you stitch across the seam allowance on the bottom side. This prevents the unseen, bottom seam allowance from misbehaving.

Careful planning will enable you to oppose seams perfectly in many neighboring units so that the joints will fall in place quite naturally. Seam allowances remain free to be creased to either side until they are crossed by another seam. Therefore, before crossing any seam with another, think first about which way you will want to crease the allowance. Keep in mind the way that you have already pressed seams (or plan to press them) in neighboring units. Finger-press accordingly.

Whenever possible, press seams the direction they are inclined to go naturally. If a bulky joint forces the seam allowance away from the joint, press it that way unless there is some overriding reason to press it the other direction.

If you find that you have stitched across a seam allowance folded the wrong way, simply release the stitches for the quarter-inch or half-inch in question, turn the seam allowances properly, and restitch. Backtack and blend the new seam into the original one.

You may have noticed how some people seem to be happy with patchwork joints that miss by a quarter-inch. Others will redo a joint when it misses by one-hundredth of an inch. Different people have different standards and different purposes. One quilter may be making a quilt to enter in a contest, in which case she may be striving for perfection. Another quilter may be making quilts to keep her children warm. She may or may not be concerned about how her joints match. Each quiltmaker must seek to please herself. She must balance her enjoyment of the work with her own satisfaction with the results. If she has to redo too many joints, she may get fed up with the project. If she doesn't take the time to do an acceptable job, she may not be happy with her quilt. Fortunately, practice makes perfect, and with experience, precise joints become easier and easier to master.

PRESSING: EXPERT ADVICE FOR MAKING YOUR SEAM ALLOWANCES BEHAVE

In all of the quilt books that are available today, very little has been written about pressing. Still, it is an important part of every successful quilt. Sometimes, the difference between a prize-winning quilt and a loser is a simple matter of pressing.

It is important to press each fabric thoroughly before cutting patches from it. All-cotton fabrics sometimes are marbled with small wrinkles after prewashing. You won't have the opportunity to press out the wrinkles after you have cut out patches, so be sure to do that before you begin. Dampen the fabric or use steam to get out every last wrinkle. Then, after you've cut the patches, take care not to rumple the fabric too much with handling.

As you join the patches together, crease the seams to one side using your thumbnail rather than using an iron. I lay the unit on my thigh, with wrong sides out and the patch toward which I will be pressing the seam allowances on top.

I then flip the top patch over so that I am looking at the right side of the unit, opened flat. I run my thumbnail along the seam line to train the seam allowance in the right direction. This is called finger-pressing. Pressing with an iron can stretch bias edges at this stage, and it should be avoided until only straight edges remain unstitched. I press my fabric before cutting patches, and I don't press with an iron again until the blocks are complete. Careful finger-pressing prevents unsightly tucks and preserves the ridges of the joints (which an iron can obliterate) to make perfectly matched joints a breeze.

Which direction is the right direction to press seam allowances? There are no hard-and-fast rules, but you'll discover some directions work better than others. Here are a few tips that my experience has taught me:

1. Generally press toward the darker fabric unless there is an overriding reason to press the other way. Usually, there isn't a problem with show-through, but pressing toward the dark will avoid any potential show-through problem that might occur.

2. Be consistent about pressing each block the same way. One exception might be to press neighboring blocks opposite ways when they will be sewn side by side. That way, seams in neighboring blocks will oppose perfectly when blocks are joined.

3. Whenever possible, press away from a bulky joint so that you don't have to fold back a many-layered seam allowance, which would make it even bulkier. For example,

if a seam joins two squares to a rectangle, press toward the rectangle. The seam allowance will be more manageable if the seam between the two squares is not folded back on itself.

4. For pinwheels or other situations where six or eight points come together, press all seams the same direction. That way, they'll oppose perfectly for the final seam across the joint and the bulk will be distributed as evenly as possible. Press the final seam open to further minimize the bulk.

5. When you are planning which way to press seam allowances, be sure to consider your quilting pattern. If any part of the quilting motif is closer to the seam line than ¼", you will want to press seams away from that area so that you won't have to quilt through bulky seam allowances.

For any other rule I devised, I found so many exceptions that the rule seemed pointless. It seems best to let you learn which way to press seam allowances from observation and experience. A few blocks are shown here from the back side so that you can study which way I pressed seam allowances. You might try making the blocks, referring to the photos as you go along. That way, you'll really understand why I pressed seams as I did.

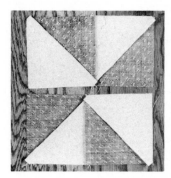

Blocks viewed from the back to show how seam allowances are pressed. Top row, left, Manhattan Block, page 30; top right, Valley of the Sun, page 26; bottom left, Country Boy, page 26; bottom right, Star Sapphire, page 24.

PARTIAL SEAMING: THE SIMPLE ALTERNATIVE TO SET-IN PATCHES

All of the blocks in this book can be made using straight seams. You won't need to cope with any tricky pivot points or with setting patches into an angle. However, a few of the patterns involve partial seaming to avoid these trickier tactics.

Partial seaming is really very simple. Just stitch a straight seam from one end of the patch to an approximate halfway point. Proceed with the rest of the block in the usual fashion. Then, when the block has progressed far enough that you can complete the seam, finish stitching the partial seam.

The hardest thing about partial seaming is knowing when to do it. This book eliminates that problem by showing you exactly when to do it in the block piecing diagrams. Each partial seam is indicated by a solid line turning into a dashed line. Where this appears, at first stitch only as far as the solid line extends. Then, after you have added the unit that has the line extending out beyond the patch, you can complete the partial seam. The partial seam, when completed, extends from the far end of the line having the extension all the way up to the point where you ended the partial seam earlier.

For example, partial seaming makes easy work of the Kitty Corner block (diagram on page 37) as follows: Start by joining B15, G2r, and G6 in the usual fashion; add B17. Make four units like this. Sew the first such unit to the A11 square with a partial seam. That is, sew halfway down the seam joining B17 to A11, as indicated by the solid line on the diagram. Leave the rest of the seam (indicated by a dashed line) free for the time being. Add the next three units,

starting in the upper right corner and proceeding clockwise. These can be stitched with complete seams from edge to edge of the patches. Fold the first unit out of the way when you attach the fourth unit. Finally, complete the partial seam joining the first unit to the A11 square and to the fourth unit.

Sometimes, a block has a number of partial seams. In each case, leave the half seam uncompleted until after the patch or unit denoted by an extended line is added.

JOINING YOUR BLOCKS INTO A QUILT TOP

Assembling Blocks in the Six Basic Sets. For blocks set side by side, the blocks are sewn together edge to edge to make straight rows. Then the rows of blocks are joined edge to edge.

For sashed sets, sashes match the block in length and they match the setting square in width. Patterns for sashes are on pages 92-97. Patterns A1, A3, A7, and A14 on pages 70-73 would make appropriate setting squares. One sashing strip is sewn between each two blocks. An extra sash is sewn to the block ends. Whole rows are made of blocks separated by strips. Sash rows are also made by joining sashes end to end with setting squares between them. Block rows are then joined with sash rows between them. An extra sash row is sewn to each end of the quilt to complete the quilt top.

For alternate block sets, you will need plain squares the same size as the blocks. Patterns for these plain squares are on pages 92-97. You will have one more block than you have plain squares. These plain squares are sewn between blocks in a checkerboard pattern. Blocks are sewn to plain squares to make rows. The first row has a block, then a plain square, then a block, and so on, ending with a block. The second row starts and ends with a plain square. Rows are joined to complete the quilt.

In a diagonal set, the rows run from corner to corner of the quilt rather than from side to side. Individual rows for a diagonally set quilt look just like rows for a straight set, with blocks joined edge to edge, except that each row ends with two large triangles. Whereas these rows are all the same length in a straight-set quilt, the rows vary in length in a diagonally set quilt.

In order to sew blocks side by side in a diagonal set, arrange the blocks on the floor, placing each at an angle with the corners of the blocks at the top, bottom, and sides of the quilt. Stand at one corner of the quilt and notice how blocks are in rows that run diagonally across the quilt. Blocks are joined edge to edge, with the first row (at one corner of the quilt) having just one block. The second row has three blocks sewn edge to edge. The third row has five blocks, and so on, with each row progressively longer. Rows taper again, getting shorter and shorter, as you approach the opposite corner of the quilt. When you have your blocks arranged on the floor, you can spread the blocks apart between rows before sewing them. This will help you see the rows. In order to square off the edges of the quilt, you will need to add large triangles, half the size of the block. For the quilt's corners, you will need triangles one-fourth the size of the block. These triangles are sewn to the ends of the rows before the rows are joined.

To make the patterns for edge triangles, trace the pattern for the square that matches the block size. Rule a diagonal from one corner to another of the square, forming two triangles. To one of the triangles, add a quarter-inch seam allowance outside the diagonal to complete a template. For the corner triangle, trace the square again. Rule two diagonals crossing at the center of the square to form four triangles. Add seam allowances to the two short edges of one triangle to make a pattern template.

Diagonal sets can also include sashes or alternate blocks. Individual rows are made just as you would make them for a straight set, with blocks' edges sewn to sashes or alternate plain squares. Lay out the blocks and the other patches on the floor, being sure to include the edge and corner triangles. Spread the blocks and patches into diagonal rows to see how to sew them together. For sashed sets, you will need small triangles half the size of the setting squares at the ends of the sash rows. Appropriate patterns for these triangles are B10, B12, B13, and B21 on pages 75-77.

Assembling Blocks in a Personal History Sampler. After you have made your blocks, arrange them on the floor, referring to your own quilt diagram or the one given on page 55. Blocks of the same size are interchangeable; try arranging and rearranging the blocks for a pleasing, balanced effect. When I made the sampler quilt shown inside the front cover, I tried to place each block near another one sharing a color in common that I could use for the strips and patches between the blocks. I made a few extra blocks from which to choose, and I ended up remaking a couple of them in different colors to achieve my desired effect. You may not need to remake any blocks if, unlike me, you had your quilt plan in mind before you started making the blocks. Leave spaces between blocks for the strips and other patches shown in your diagram.

Choosing fabrics to go with the neighboring blocks, cut out strips and patches as needed. My sampler quilt used patches A1, A4, B13, D1, D2, D11, D13, D17, D18, G5, K2, K4, K8, K10, K14, and K15 for fillers. Join the small squares, triangles, or strips into units, laying each in place on the floor as you complete it. When you have completed all of the filler units, spread the blocks and units apart in rows. Join the blocks and strips or units, picking up just the ones that you are about to stitch. After stitching, put them back in position on the floor. Join all of the blocks and units to form straight rows. Join rows. My quilt also had strips and patches forming a two-inch-wide border around the edges to complete the quilt top. Add borders to your quilt according to your plan.

QUILTING

Once you have completed your quilt top and added the desired borders, you will want to give it one last, good pressing. Pick off or snip any stray threads. Now, if you haven't already planned it, it's time to think about the quilting. There are four basic kinds of quilting, as follows:

1. In-the-Ditch Quilting. This quilting is directly beside the seam lines on the side without the seam allowances. In-the-ditch quilting is done "by eye," without marking. It can be a little tough to manipulate the fabric onto the needle so close to bulky seam allowances, and you will have to cross over thick seam allowances at joints. This makes it a little harder to make perfect stitches when you are quilting in the ditch, but being so close to the seam lines, the stitches tend to be barely visible, so any flaws are minimized.

In-the-Ditch Quilting   *Outline Quilting*

2. Outline Quilting. This also follows the seam lines. However, it is done one-fourth-inch from the seams, just beyond the seam allowances. Since outline quilting is done around each patch, there are two lines of quilting for each seam, one on each side of it. This makes for almost twice as much quilting as there would be in the ditch. However, you won't need to cross any bulky seam allowances, and the stitching is a little faster and easier. Outline quilting shows up much better than in-the-ditch quilting, so you'll want to have small, even stitches. Outline quilting can be done "by eye" or along the edge of one-quarter-inch masking tape placed beside the seam. It is not necessary to mark the quilting before basting; simply lay down the tape (one strip at a time) after the quilt is installed in the hoop or frame. To proceed from quilting one patch to another, pass the needle into the batting for a half-inch and bring it up in the neighboring patch to start quilting there.

3. Marked Motifs. Alternate plain blocks, borders, sashes, and large patches are often decorated with marked motifs that run the gamut from simple to elaborate. Feathers, cables, and flowers are among the favorites. A number of suitable motifs are on pages 92-97. Marking the motifs takes some care, but quilting them is easy and the results are splendid. Mark these motifs before basting the quilt top to the batting and lining. To do this, you can position a slotted stencil over the quilt and pencil through the slots, or you can position the quilt over a black-marker drawing of the motif and trace onto the quilt top with a pencil.

Marked Quilting   *Filler Quilting*

4. Filler Quilting. Background patterns of interlocked circles, clamshells, grids of squares, parallel lines, or random stippling are used to fill in areas around more fanciful motifs. They serve to depress the surrounding area, making the more important motifs puff up. Straight lines can be marked with masking tape as you quilt or ruled and marked with a pencil before basting. Clamshells and other designs based on circles can be marked with a pencil using an appropriate-sized cup, saucer, or jar as a template. Mark these before basting layers. Filler quilting is time-consuming, but it adds a finished look to a quilt. In times past, when cotton batting required close quilting to stay put, filler quilting was the rule. Nowadays, quilters often forgo it, since polyester batts don't need to be so firmly anchored. Still, some of the best quilts being made today boast fine filler quilting.

Before you can start quilting, you must prepare the layers. Seam together the necessary lengths of fabric to make a lining at least four inches larger all around than the top of the quilt. Press the lining, pressing seam allowances to one side. Lay the lining face down on the floor, ping-pong table, or other suitably large surface. Smooth the batting over the lining, trimming the excess batting roughly even with the lining. Center the quilt top, face up, over the batting. Baste the layers together with inch-long stitches in lines four to six inches apart. Mount the quilt in a hoop or frame. It needn't be drum tight, but it shouldn't be entirely slack, either.

Now you are ready to begin quilting. If you have never watched an experienced quilter at work, try to arrange to do so. Many beginners are surprised when they first observe the technique. It helps to see someone doing it comfortably, especially since it may feel totally unnatural to you at first. By watching an experienced quilter you'll also have some idea of what stitch length is appropriate. The finest quilters today and in the past have managed perfect, even stitches, fifteen to twenty to the inch, counting stitches on the face of the quilt only. Many quilters are satisfied with six or eight stitches to the inch. I think that most contemporary quilters aim for ten to fifteen stitches per inch now. Of course, your stitches may be longer than you'd like at first, but they will improve with time. What is most important at first is using the proper technique. Without that, your quilting may never improve.

A self-taught quilter once did a small quilting project for me. It was obvious that she took pride in her work. Her stitches were perfectly even, but they were a quarter-inch long and a quarter-inch apart. I asked her to demonstrate how she quilted. She produced a long needle, which she held between her thumb and forefinger, and proceeded to stitch as if she were basting. When I showed her a few pointers and gave her a #10 betweens needle, she was able to quilt ten stitches per inch right away. It may not be quite that easy for you, but do try the proper technique.

Cut off a 24″ to 36″ length of quilting thread. Thread a short needle (#8-12 betweens) with it. The thread should be a single strand with no knot. Take a stitch along the marked quilting line. Pull the thread to its halfway point, leaving a 12″ or 18″ tail free. Take short running stitches

through all layers. The stitches should be the same length on the top and bottom surfaces of the quilt. Don't grasp the needle between your thumb and index finger; instead, push the needle from the eye end with a thimble on your middle finger. If you are right handed, use your right thumb to depress the fabric in front of the needle, and use your left thumb and middle finger below the quilt to help guide the fabric onto the needle. This will probably feel awkward at first, especially if you are not accustomed to using a thimble. However, it is worth getting used to this method, since your fingers will get painfully sore without a thimble, and you will have difficulty achieving the desired short, even sititches unless you rock the needle from the end in this way.

When you reach the end of the thread, take a small backstitch. Then run the needle through the batting to a nearby seam line and take a small stitch right in the valley of the seam line; it will not be visible. Run the thread back in the

opposite direction, along the seam line and between layers, for an inch or so. Bring the needle back out. Snip the thread directly at the surface of the quilt top and let the thread end slip back between the layers. Thread the remaining half of the first length of thread into the needle, and continue quilting.

BINDING & FINISHING

When the quilting is completed, trim the lining and batting exactly even with the quilt top. Remove the basting stitches.

Cut a straight binding strip for each side of the quilt, with strips 1¾″ wide and about two inches longer than the corresponding edge of the quilt. Press each strip in half lengthwise with right sides out.

Pin a binding strip to one edge of the quilt, with both

long raw edges of the doubled binding strip even with the raw edges of the quilt top, batting, and lining. Trim off the excess length of the binding ¼″ beyond the raw edge of the quilt top and turn under the extra at both ends. Stitch through all layers in a ¼″ seam. Roll the binding to the back side. Pin, aligning the fold of the binding with the line of

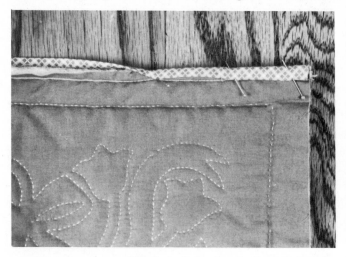

stitching just sewn. Blindstitch by hand. Repeat for the opposite edge. For the last two edges, turn under the ends of the binding strips to be even with the binding already sewn. Stitch and roll, as before. If desired, you can turn under the excess at an angle for these last two strips to simulate a mitered corner.

Embroider your name and the date as a perfect finishing touch.

Judy's Star, B24, pgs. 36 & 56

September Star, D35, pgs. 36 & 56

Writer's Block, D35, pgs. 36 & 56

Eyes of Blue, C35, pgs. 36 & 56

Motown Sounds, C35, pgs. 36 & 56

Bonny Scotland, C29, pgs. 36 & 56

Diamond Jubilee, C35, pgs. 37 & 56

Aloha, B23, pgs. 37 & 56

March Winds, C35, pgs. 37 & 56

Land of Lincoln, C29, pgs. 37 & 56

Windy City, C23, pgs. 37 & 56

Saturday Afternoon, B23, pgs. 37 & 56

See page 35 for explanation of page references and pattern ratings for captions below color photos.

All That Jazz, C35, pgs. 37 & 56

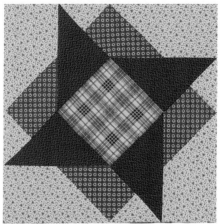

Kitty Corner, D30, pgs. 37 & 56

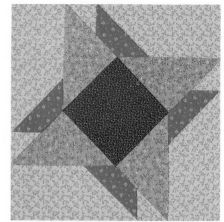

Wheat Field, D30, pgs. 37 & 56

Baker's Dozen, C59, pgs. 38 & 56

Wild Irish Rose, B42, pgs. 38 & 57

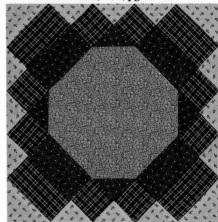

Ellis Island Block, B53, pgs. 38 & 57

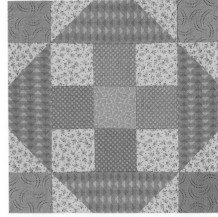

Santa Fe Trail, B36, pgs. 38 & 57

Philadelphia Pavement, B30, pgs. 38 & 57. Alternate block set, diagonal.

City Block, A24, pgs. 38 & 57

Hero's Welcome, C48, pgs. 38 & 57

Memory Block, D76, pgs. 38 & 57

November Nights, C40, pgs. 38 & 57

Country French, B48, pgs. 39 & 57

Silver Screen, B53, pgs. 39 & 57

China Doll, B76, pgs. 39 & 57

Sunday Best, A53, pgs. 39 & 57

California Dreamin', B71, pgs. 39 & 57

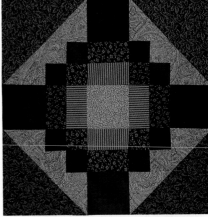

Wall Street, B59, pgs. 39 & 57

Stitcher's Square, A65, pgs. 39 & 57

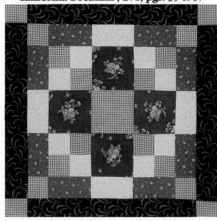

Chocolate Lover, A65, pgs. 39 & 57

Bookworm, B53, pgs. 39 & 57

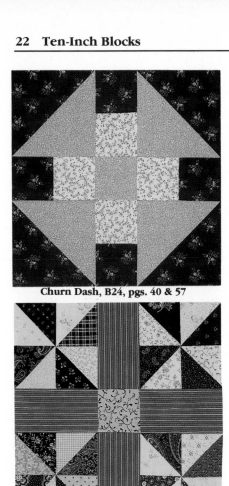

Churn Dash, B24, pgs. 40 & 57

Sister's Choice, B48, pgs. 40 & 57

Country Life, B36, pgs. 40 & 57

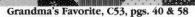

Grandma's Favorite, C53, pgs. 40 & 58

Duck & Ducklings, B36, pgs. 40 & 58

Cross & Crown, B42, pgs. 40 & 58

Duck Paddle, B48, pgs. 40 & 58

Jack in the Box, B42, pgs. 40 & 58

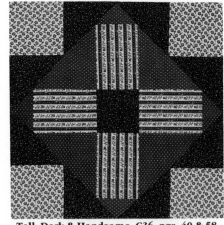

Tall, Dark & Handsome, C36, pgs. 40 & 58

Brotherly Love, B24, pgs. 41 & 58

Roman Holiday, B48, pgs. 41 & 58

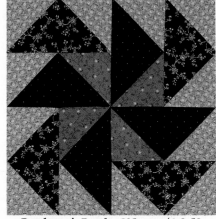

Dutchman's Puzzle, C35, pgs. 41 & 58

Martha's Vineyard, C37, pgs. 41 & 58. Five blocks are set diagonally with sashes.

Short & Sweet, C25, pgs. 41 & 58

December Days, C28, pgs. 41 & 58

City of Angels, C37, pgs. 41 & 58

April Showers, B33, pgs. 41 & 58

Pride of Ohio, C49, pgs. 41 & 58

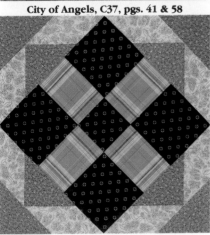

Block & Tackle, B25, pgs. 42 & 58

Beach Party, C37, pgs. 42 & 58

Puppy Love, C37, pgs. 42 & 58

Skyrocket, C29, pgs. 42 & 58

Kentucky Bluegrass, C37, pgs. 42 & 58

Washington Monument, C37, pgs. 42 & 59

Georgia Peach, C37, pgs. 42 & 59

Star Sapphire, C41, pgs. 42 & 59

Royal Star Quilt, B29, pgs. 42 & 59

Roll On, Columbia, C61, pgs. 43 & 59

Kissin' Cousins, C33, pgs. 43 & 59

Broadway Nights, C33, pgs. 43 & 59

Children of Israel, B33, pgs. 43 & 59

Hawkeye Block, C37, pgs. 43 & 59

Monday's Child, C33, pgs. 43 & 59

Surf's Up, B33, pgs. 43 & 59

Emerald Isle, C37, pgs. 43 & 59

Baltimore Oriole, B29, pgs. 43 & 59. Five blocks are set straight with alternate plain squares.

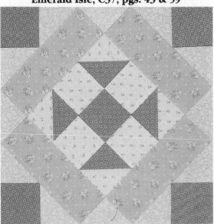

Baby's Breath, B33, pgs. 44 & 59

Setting Sail, C40, pgs. 44 & 59

Boy's Nonsense, B17, pgs. 44 & 59

Mexican Star, B33, pgs. 44 & 59

Denver Mint, B25, pgs. 44 & 59

London Bridge, B37, pgs. 44 & 59

Star & Cross, B29, pgs. 44 & 59

Country Boy, B45, pgs. 44 & 60

Springfield, B29, pgs. 44 & 60

Song & Dance, C37, pgs. 45 & 60

Grand Canyon Suite, C41, pgs. 45 & 60

June Bride, C29, pgs. 45 & 60

Auntie's Favorite, C45, pgs. 45 & 60

Valley of the Sun, C33, pgs. 45 & 60

Swing in the Center, C33, pgs. 45 & 60

Home Grown, B25, pgs. 45 & 60

Octoberfest, B24, pgs. 45 & 60

Chinatown, C45, pgs. 45 & 60

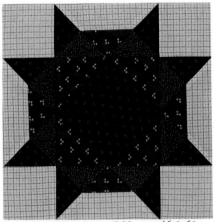

Georgetown Loop, D33, pgs. 46 & 60

Sparks Flyin', C33, pgs. 46 & 60

Martha Washington Star, C28, pgs. 46 & 60

Taj Mahal, B33, pgs. 46 & 60

The Royal Mile, C41, pgs. 46 & 60

Independence Block, B25, pgs. 46 & 60

The Railroad Quilt, B32, pgs. 46 & 60

Hoosier Block, C33, pgs. 46 & 60

Green-Eyed Lady, B25, pgs. 46 & 60. Nine blocks are set straight side by side.

Smoky Mountain Block, B25, pgs. 47 & 61

Weathervane, C37, pgs. 47 & 61

African Safari, C41, pgs. 47 & 61

Cajun Spice, B25, pgs. 47 & 61

Oregon Trail, B25, pgs. 47 & 61

Grand Prix, C37, pgs. 47 & 61

Florida Oranges, C45, pgs. 47 & 61

Prairie Nine-Patch, C37, pgs. 47 & 61

May Flowers, C45, pgs. 47 & 61

St. Lawrence Seaway, C41, pgs. 48 & 61

Daddy's Little Girl, D21, pgs. 48 & 61

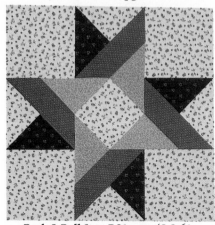

Rock & Roll Star, D21, pgs. 48 & 61

Land of the Midnight Sun, D29, pgs. 48 & 61

Black Forest Torte, D25, pgs. 48 & 61

Baseball Star, C25, pgs. 48 & 61

January Thaw, C29, pgs. 48 & 61

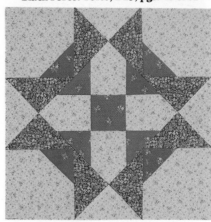

Golden Gate, B29, pgs. 48 & 61

Vive la France, C61, pgs. 48 & 61

Guitar Picker, C60, pgs. 49 & 61

Carolina in the Morning, C45, pgs. 49 & 61

American Beauty, C41, pgs. 49 & 62

San Diego Sunshine, B41, pgs. 49 & 62

Truck Stop, B49, pgs. 49 & 62

Spanish Moss, C48, pgs. 49 & 62

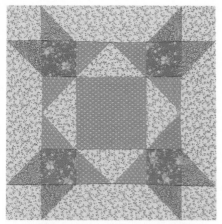

Cottage Garden, C33, pgs. 49 & 62

Rabbit's Paw, B25, pgs. 49 & 62. Nine blocks are set straight with sashes.

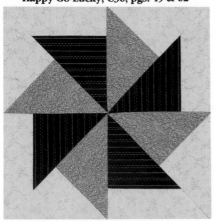

Happy-Go-Lucky, C36, pgs. 49 & 62

Pinwheel, B16, pgs. 50 & 62

Shopping Spree, B20, pgs. 50 & 62

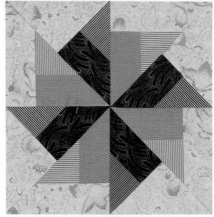

Kindred Spirits, B24, pgs. 50 & 62

Mississippi Queen, B20, pgs. 50 & 62

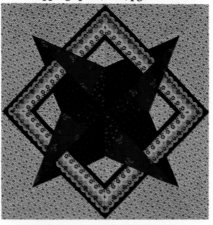

Mother's Day, C44, pgs. 50 & 62

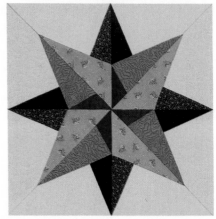

Manhattan Block, C28, pgs. 50 & 62

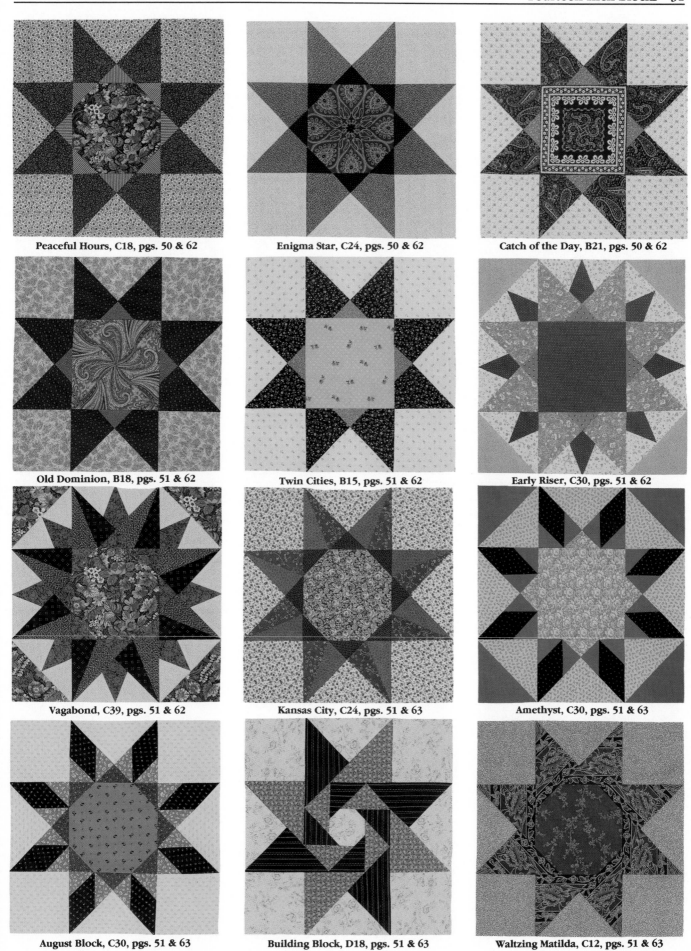

Peaceful Hours, C18, pgs. 50 & 62

Enigma Star, C24, pgs. 50 & 62

Catch of the Day, B21, pgs. 50 & 62

Old Dominion, B18, pgs. 51 & 62

Twin Cities, B15, pgs. 51 & 62

Early Riser, C30, pgs. 51 & 62

Vagabond, C39, pgs. 51 & 62

Kansas City, C24, pgs. 51 & 63

Amethyst, C30, pgs. 51 & 63

August Block, C30, pgs. 51 & 63

Building Block, D18, pgs. 51 & 63

Waltzing Matilda, C12, pgs. 51 & 63

Dear Old Dad, C45, pgs. 52 & 63. Thirteen blocks are set diagonally side by side.

Union Block, B18, pgs. 52 & 63

Tuesday's Child, C21, pgs. 52 & 63

Rocky Mountain High, C24, pgs. 52 & 63

Baby Boomer, C27, pgs. 52 & 63

Orient Express, C24, pgs. 52 & 63

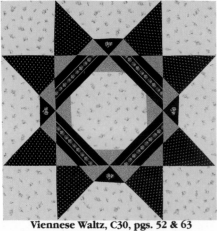

Viennese Waltz, C30, pgs. 52 & 63

Celtic Block, C33, pgs. 52 & 63

Southern Belle, C33, pgs. 52 & 63

Patience Patchwork, B57, pgs. 53 & 63

Whistling Dixie, C39, pgs. 53 & 63

Night Owl, B33, pgs. 53 & 63

Girl Next Door, B24, pgs. 53 & 63

Ozark Beauty, C39, pgs 53 & 63

Texas Two-Step, C30, pgs. 53 & 63

Fourth of July, C30, pgs. 53 & 64

Sunny Side Up, B33, pgs. 53 & 64

Puppy Dog Tails, B27, pgs. 53 & 64

Brown-Eyed Susan, C36, pgs. 54 & 64

Gramp's Block, C36, pgs. 54 & 64

Puget Sound, B27, pgs. 54 & 64

Bear's Foot, B33, pgs. 54 & 64

Bear's Paw, B36, pgs. 54 & 64

Calgary Stampede, C39, pgs. 54 & 64

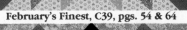

February's Finest, C39, pgs. 54 & 64

Norwegian Wood, C45, pgs. 54 & 64

Merry Olde England, C30, pgs. 54 & 64

Ontario Lakes, C30, pgs. 55 & 64

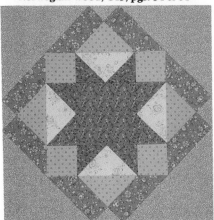

Collector's Block, C27, pgs. 55 & 64

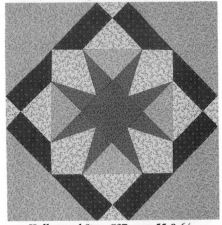

Hollywood Star, C27, pgs. 55 & 64

Taos Treasure, C36, pgs. 55 & 64

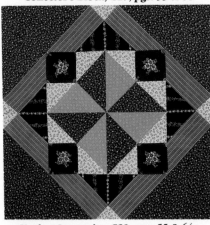

Yankee Ingenuity, C29, pgs. 55 & 64

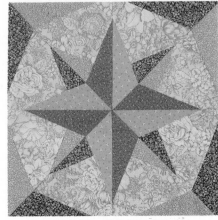

Teacher's Pet, C24, pgs. 55 & 64

THE BLOCK COLLECTION

For each of the 174 blocks in the book, there is a color photograph, a block diagram with description, and a coloring book drawing. The ten-inch blocks are presented first, followed by the twelve- and fourteen-inch blocks. Similar blocks are grouped together so that you may better observe their differences. Blocks appear in the same sequence in all three sections, and page numbers for the other two sections are listed in each caption to make it easy for you to locate the material you seek.

Color photographs are on pages 19-34. Below each photo is the block name followed by the pattern rating and the page numbers for the diagram and the coloring book drawing. Diagrams and descriptions are on pages 36-55. Captions here include name, block size, page numbers for the color photograph and coloring book drawing, and setting suggestions and helpful hints. Coloring book drawings are on pages 56-64. Captions include name and page numbers for the color photograph and diagram.

Explanation of Pattern Ratings. Patterns are rated for ease of construction, using a scale from A (easiest) to E (most difficult). None of the patterns in this book is hard enough to rate an "E," which would involve curves, very sharp points, set-in patches, or more than eight points converging. Consider patterns rated "C" to be average. An "A" rating was given to the simplest of blocks, those made entirely from squares and rectangles. A "B" rating indicates a very easy block having some right triangles. A "C" block is a typical block. It may have a variety of shapes to assemble in a number of units, but the construction is generally straightforward. A "D" block has more joints to match, more bias edges, or partial seaming. The "D" blocks may require some concentration. Although they are not exceptionally difficult, the "D" blocks might be a challenge for beginners until they have gained some confidence in their patchwork skills.

Pattern ratings also include a numerical designation. This indicates the number of patches per square foot that the pattern involves. For 12″ blocks, the number is the same as the number of patches in the block. For 10″ or 14″ blocks, the number of patches is adjusted by the proper factor to account for the size differences. The assigned numbers, then, can be readily compared. Numbers for the blocks in this book range from 12 to 76; 35 patches per square foot is the average for the blocks in this book. Seventy percent of the blocks here fall in the range of 20-39 patches per square foot. The higher the number, the more time and patience will be required to make the quilt.

BLOCK DIAGRAMS & DESCRIPTIONS

This section contains piecing diagrams, block sizes, setting suggestions, and helpful hints for each of the 174 blocks. To the right of the block name are two page numbers, the first for the color photograph of the block and the second for the blank block drawing.

How to Read the Diagrams. Letters in the diagrams on pages 36-55 refer to the full-size pattern pieces on pages 70-97. The drawings show not only the patch letters, but also the piecing sequence. The first patches to be sewn together are shown already joined into rows or other units. These units are then joined to make larger units until the last units are joined to complete the block. Join the units that are shown closest to each other first. The diagrams often show units completely exploded in one corner, with each progressive corner having the units joined one step further. A dashed line in the diagram is used to indicate a partial seam. The dashed end of the seam should be left free until after the unit

indicated by an extended line is added. Then the partial seam can be completed.

A pattern letter followed by an "r" indicates that the patch is the reverse of the pattern given in the book. Turn the pattern face down on the fabric to cut reverses.

A Word About the Descriptions. As I made the blocks in this book, some tips came to mind that you might appreciate. I have included these in the block descriptions. Some of the tips refer to specific colors and fabrics used in the samples shown in the color photographs.

Quilt Sets. Every block in the book is suitable to be made into a quilt. The six basic arrangements for blocks (called "sets") are shown in color photographs on pages 20, 23, 25, 27, 30, and 32. The description given by each block in this section suggests a suitable quilt arrangement. However, feel free to set your blocks in any arrangement that you desire.

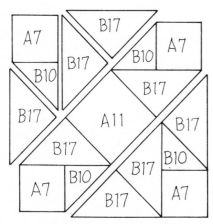

Judy's Star, 10″, pgs. 19 & 56

This easy-to-make block looks pretty set with sashes or alternate blocks. Choose two shades of one color for the points to give the star a three-dimensional appearance.

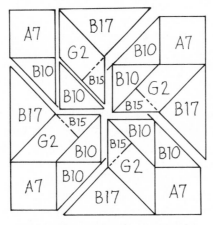

September Star, 10″, pgs. 19 & 56

An intriguing mix of a star and pinwheel, this pattern is perfect for sashed sets, either straight or on the diagonal. Partial seaming permits you to make this block without setting in any patches.

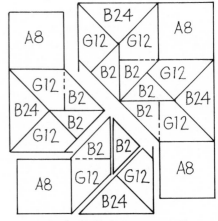

Writer's Block, 10″, pgs. 19 & 56

This block was inspired by September Star, at left, but looks different made with true diamonds. Partial seaming makes it possible to sew the block with no fussy angles. Set it diagonally with alternate plain blocks for a pretty quilt.

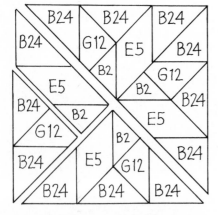

Eyes of Blue, 10″, pgs. 19 & 56

This is similar to Writer's Block, but it is even easier to make. Set straight with sashes, this block has a traditional look. Select a striped fabric for the background triangles to create a framed effect.

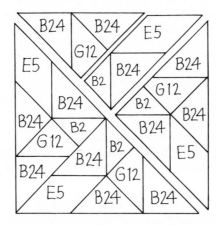

Motown Sounds, 10″, pgs. 19 & 56

This Supreme block is a real Temptation to make. The pinwheel spins in triplicate for a lively look. Set the blocks side by side and you'll see additional pinwheels form at the block corners.

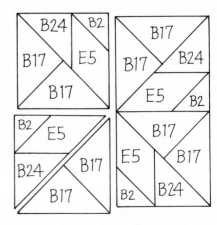

Bonny Scotland, 10″, pgs. 19 & 56

The colors of highland heather define this pretty pinwheel. Set blocks with 2″ sashes for a traditional-style quilt. Press seams all the same direction for a perfect match at the center joint; then press the last, long seam open.

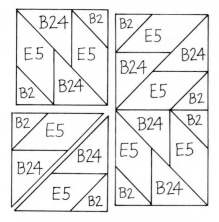

Diamond Jubilee, 10″, pgs. 19 & 56

Set straight with blocks side by side, you'll see a secondary pattern of pinwheels form where the blocks touch. This is lovely in two colors as well as in several shades of the same color.

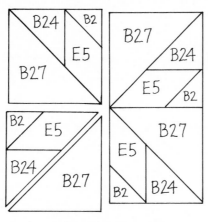

Aloha, 10″, pgs. 19 & 56

This quick-and-easy pattern looks especially handsome with blocks set side by side on the diagonal. Press seams all the same direction to oppose perfectly at the center joint. After stitching the last seam, press that seam open.

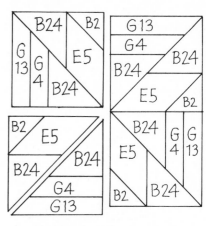

March Winds, 10″, pgs. 19 & 56

I like this block set straight with dark sashes. Notice the linear print in the light background. When you work with a print like this, try cutting half the background patches on the lengthwise grain and half crosswise, as I have done here.

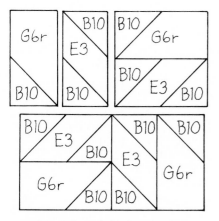

Land of Lincoln, 10″, pgs. 19 & 56

Set blocks straight with sashing for a most traditional effect. Two shades of the same color add interest to the motif.

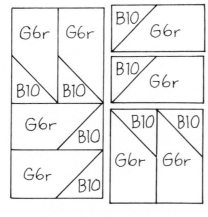

Windy City, 10″, pgs. 19 & 56

This pinwheel is a breeze to make. Set the blocks straight, either side by side or with sashes. The rhombus shapes are ideal for striped fabrics.

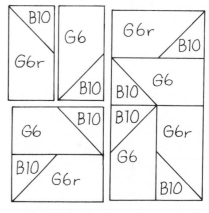

Saturday Afternoon, 10″, pgs. 19 & 56

Border stripes in the background give this block its distinctive look. Set blocks with alternate plain squares for a sweet quilt that you can make in a jiffy.

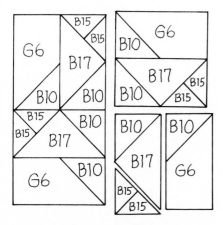

All That Jazz, 10″, pgs. 20 & 56

This block will strike a responsive chord with jazz fanciers. It is an easy-to-sew pattern that gains punch from the use of stripes and brilliant colors. Blocks set straight with sashes would make a wonderful quilt.

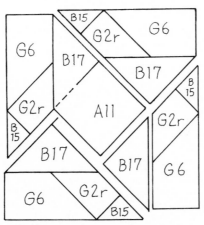

Kitty Corner, 10″, pgs. 20 & 56

This block creates the same basic image as All That Jazz, but without the stripes it can be done with fewer patches. Partial seaming keeps the sewing straightforward. Set straight with sashes, a pleasant old-fashioned quilt results.

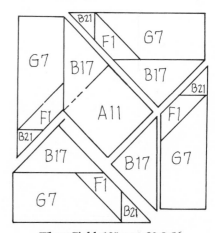

Wheat Field, 10″, pgs. 20 & 56

This block is best set straight with sashes. Two shades of one color give the star points a three-dimensional quality. Partial seaming is a helpful skill here.

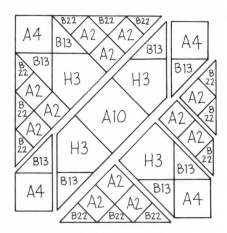

Baker's Dozen, 10″, pgs. 20 & 56

Twelve small squares make up the dozen here, with one large square as the baker's bonus. Set blocks straight with narrow sashes for a quilt with old-time charm.

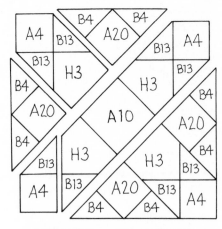

Wild Irish Rose, 10″, pgs. 20 & 57

Set this block straight with alternate plain blocks for an attractive quilt that is a cinch to make. Luck of the Irish!

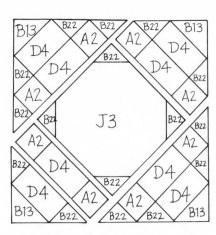

Ellis Island Block, 10″, pgs. 20 & 57

This block honors the emigrants who left their homelands to be a part of this great country. Set blocks straight with alternate plain blocks for a quilt with plenty of space for lavish quilting.

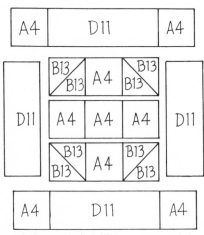

Philadelphia Pavement, 10″, pgs. 20 & 57

Blocks can be set straight or diagonally—with sashes, alternate blocks or just side by side—for totally different looks.

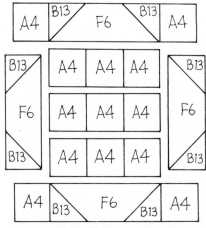

Santa Fe Trail, 10″, pgs. 20 & 57

Southwestern colors give this block a Native American look. I like Santa Fe Trail set with two-inch-wide sashes. Be sure to keep the colors soft for a sun-bleached desert feeling.

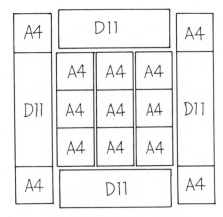

City Block, 10″, pgs. 20 & 57

I couldn't find this pattern in any of my sources, but it's so basic that I can't believe it hasn't been done before. I call it City Block for its concrete-and-steel colors. In any set, this would make a handsome, yet makeable quilt.

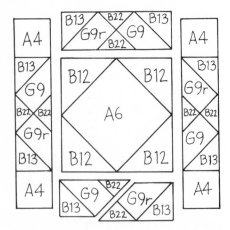

Hero's Welcome, 10″, pgs. 21 & 57

Stripes enhance this design and add a medallion-like luster. Set blocks alternately with plain squares for relief.

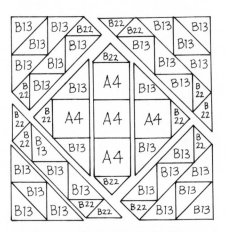

Memory Block, 10″, pgs. 21 & 57

Sign your name in the center square for a great block to exchange. Set straight with two-inch sashes for an unforgettable old-fashioned quilt.

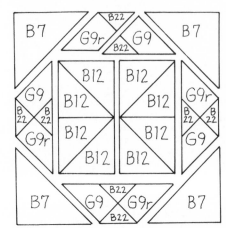

November Nights, 10″, pgs. 21 & 57

I think this block is lovely set straight with narrow sashes. Cool colors and swirly motifs suggest snowdrifts and a wintry peace.

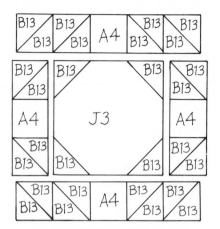

Country French, 10″, pgs. 21 & 57

Set this block with wide, floral striped sashes to complete the country look. Wouldn't a quilt like this befit a rustic pine bedroom set?

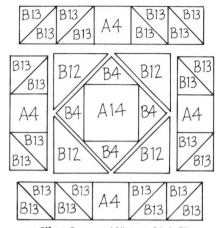

Silver Screen, 10″, pgs. 21 & 57

For best performance by a block in a straight set, choose Silver Screen set with alternate plain squares. For crisp points, press seams outward from the center.

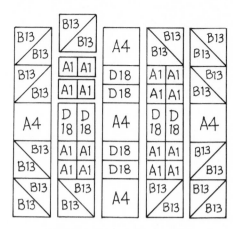

China Doll, 10″, pgs. 21 & 57

This is a simplified version of a traditional Young Man's Fancy block. Set blocks straight with sashing for a pleasantly rhythmic pattern.

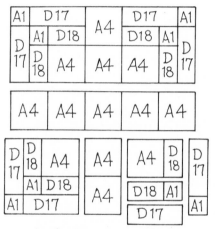

Sunday Best, 10″, pgs. 21 & 57

A charming block with a somewhat Victorian flavor, thanks to the rose floral print. Set with two-inch sashes in white or black prints for two totally different looks. Press all seams outward from the center, as you would a Log Cabin.

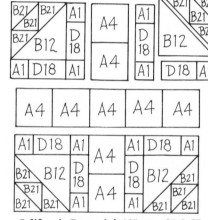

California Dreamin', 10″, pgs. 21 & 57

Fields of poppies and blue Pacific skies are reflected in this unusual design. Set blocks straight with two-inch sashes of blue.

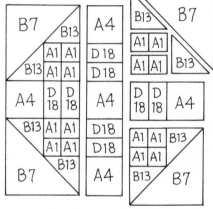

Wall Street, 10″, pgs. 21 & 57

The future looks bullish for this good-looking block. Make blocks from different scrap fabrics and set them side by side for an easy-to-make quilt.

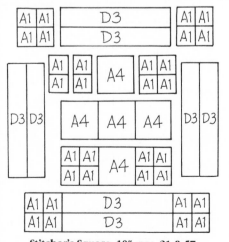

Stitcher's Square, 10″, pgs. 21 & 57

Set straight with either one-inch or two-inch sashes, this quilt would look wonderfully complex. Of course, the sewing is really perfectly simple. Tea-colored muslin gives the block an antique appearance.

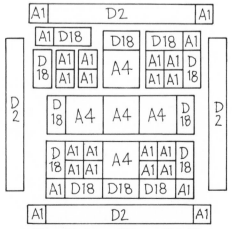

Chocolate Lover, 10″, pgs. 21 & 57

Set with one-inch sashes of dark brown, Chocolate Lover makes a delectable quilt. The patches are small and numerous, but the sewing is exceptionally easy. This pattern lends itself to many speed techniques and shortcuts.

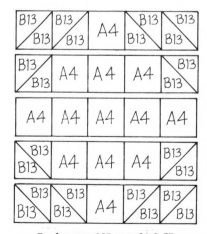

Bookworm, 10″, pgs. 21 & 57

Set with alternate plain blocks and richly quilted with a fluid, curving design, this quilt is a real beauty. Anyone would enjoy curling up with a Bookworm quilt!

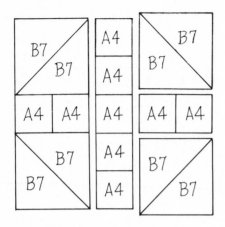

Churn Dash, 10″, pgs. 22 & 57

Churn Dash is a favorite traditional design, this time made from German dirndl fabric. I like this simple block set straight with sashes or alternate blocks.

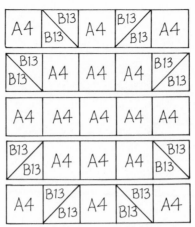

Sister's Choice, 10″, pgs. 22 & 57

One of the simplest and most handsome of traditional designs, Sister's Choice looks great set straight or diagonally, with sashes or alternate blocks.

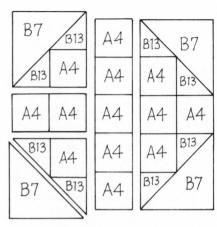

Country Life, 10″, pgs. 22 & 57

As easy as pie—and just as hard to resist, this block is perfect for scraps. Set the blocks straight with plaid sashes for a down-home country quilt.

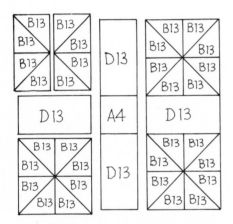

Grandma's Favorite, 10″, pgs. 22 & 58

This design is wonderful in scraps. Set it straight or on the diagonal with alternate plain blocks or sashes. With its old-fashioned charm, you can see why Grandma would like it.

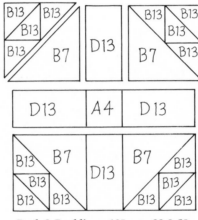

Duck & Ducklings, 10″, pgs. 22 & 58

No ugly duckling, this block! It's pretty right from the start. Set blocks with sashes or alternate plain squares for a quick-and-easy quilt. Press all seams away from the pink B13 triangles for the smoothest patchwork.

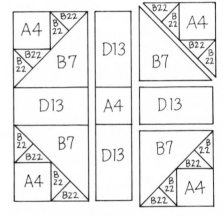

Cross & Crown, 10″, pgs. 22 & 58

This block was a favorite of mine when I was a beginning quilter. It looks good and goes together quickly when set on the diagonal with alternate plain blocks.

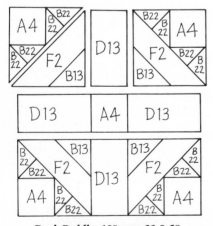

Duck Paddle, 10″, pgs. 22 & 58

Here is another traditional favorite. Try setting this block with two-inch-wide sashes. I especially like this block on the diagonal.

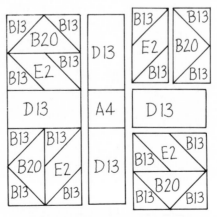

Jack in the Box, 10″, pgs. 22 & 58

This design can look quaint or contemporary, depending on your fabric choices. Two shades of a single color lend dimensionality to this whirligig pattern. Set blocks straight with sashes, pressing seams toward the sashes.

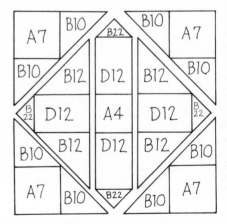

Tall, Dark & Handsome, 10″, pgs. 22 & 58

You'll want to make a date with this block. For a striking, traditional-style quilt, set blocks on the diagonal with alternate plain squares. Stripes enhance the central motif.

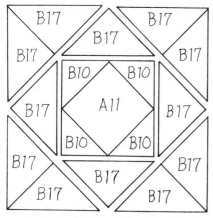

Brotherly Love, 10″, pgs. 22 & 58

Stripes frame this simple design and give it an air of distinction. Set blocks straight or diagonally with alternate plain blocks. Press all seam allowances outward from the center.

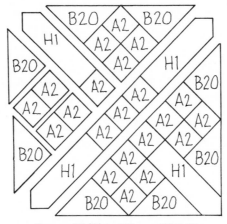

Roman Holiday, 10″, pgs. 22 & 58

Colored like the Italian flag, this block looks festive and spirited. I prefer this pattern set with narrow sashes of red. Press seam allowances toward the sashes.

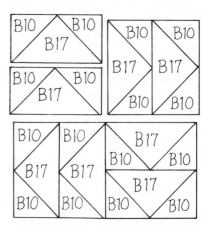

Dutchman's Puzzle, 10″, pgs. 22 & 58

This pattern looks good in any set. The sewing will be easier with sashes or alternate blocks rather than a side-by-side set, however. Press seams toward the small triangles in each three-triangle unit. When joining the units, press toward the base of the large triangle.

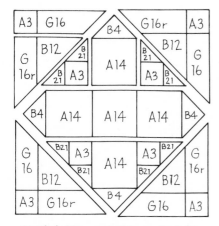

Martha's Vineyard, 12″, pgs. 23 & 58

This block is stunning set with sashes. Cut B12 and B21 triangles with their long edges on the straight grain.

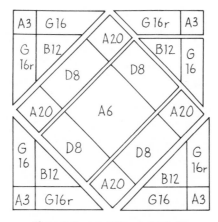

Short & Sweet, 12″, pgs. 23 & 58

Make blocks from a variety of scrap fabrics and set them side by side for a pleasant all-over pattern.

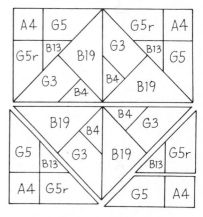

December Days, 12″, pgs. 23 & 58

Set blocks straight with one- or two-inch sashes for a simply striking quilt.

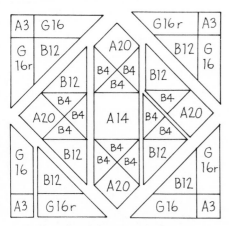

City of Angels, 12″, pgs. 23 & 58

Lovely pastel colors give this block a delicate appeal. Set blocks alternately with lavishly quilted plain squares for a truly heavenly quilt.

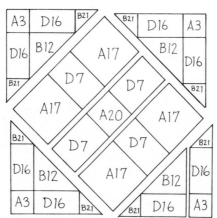

April Showers, 12″, pgs. 23 & 58

Set this block with one-and-one-half-inch sashes for a pleasant, springtime quilt.

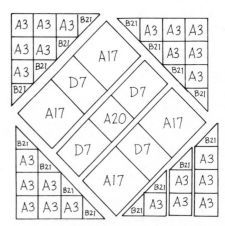

Pride of Ohio, 12″, pgs. 23 & 58

Subtle color gradations give this block its luminosity and elegance. Set blocks straight with sashes for a stunning quilt.

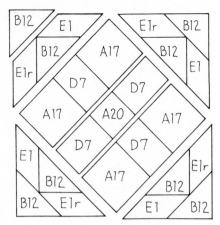

Block & Tackle, 12″, pgs. 23 & 58

A handsome design for a fisherman or football buff, this pattern uses a shirting plaid to set a masculine tone. Set blocks with sashes or alternate plain blocks for a great quilt.

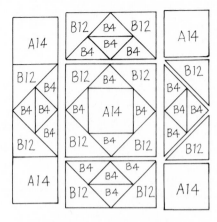

Beach Party, 12″, pgs. 23 & 58

Surf and sand colors lend a summery quality to this block. Set blocks diagonally with alternate plain blocks for a pleasing effect. Press seams away from the center square.

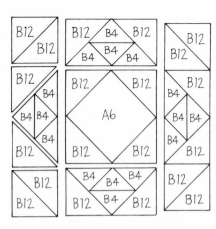

Puppy Love, 12″, pgs. 23 & 58

Choose scraps for a playful touch. A straight set with wide sashes will complete the old-fashioned look.

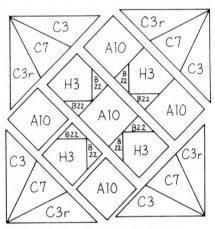

Skyrocket, 12″, pgs. 24 & 58

Make a dazzling quilt of Skyrocket blocks set straight with alternate plain squares. For best results, follow the light-medium-dark values as in the photo. Choose a monochromatic color scheme or two or three colors, as desired.

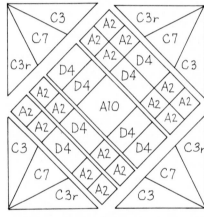

Kentucky Bluegrass, 12″, pgs. 24 & 58

This block is a thoroughbred. Set the blocks together with narrow sashing, and the neighboring blocks will interact for a pleasant effect. This set lets you assemble the quilt without having to match points of neighboring blocks.

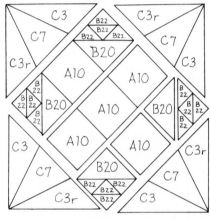

Washington Monument, 12″, pgs. 24 & 59

The shapes in the corners reminded me of the Washington Monument, thus the name. I like this block set diagonally with alternate plain blocks.

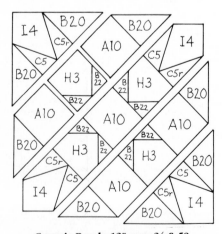

Georgia Peach, 12″, pgs. 24 & 59

This luscious block is pretty set straight with sashing. The cut-off points of C5 and I4 patches will guide you in aligning the patches perfectly for seaming.

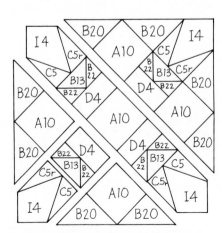

Star Sapphire, 12″, pgs. 24 & 59

This block makes a gem of a quilt set straight with sashing. Press B seam allowances toward D's, and press I4's toward C5's.

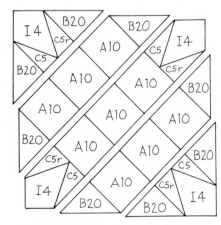

Royal Star Quilt, 12″, pgs. 24 & 59

Press I4-C5 seam allowances toward A10 and press A10 toward B20 for the smoothest possible block. Set blocks straight with blue alternate blocks for a princely, but easy, quilt.

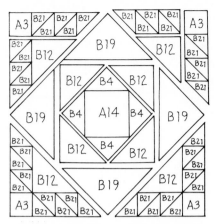

Roll On, Columbia, 12″, pgs. 24 & 59

This makes an attractive monochromatic block. For a crisper look, choose prints that are less busy. Set blocks diagonally with alternate plain blocks for relief.

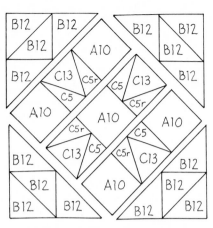

Kissin' Cousins, 12″, pgs. 24 & 59

Set blocks with bright sashes for a cheery quilt. Press seam allowances away from the central star for crisp points.

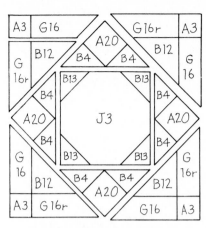

Broadway Nights, 12″, pgs. 24 & 59

Set with narrow, black sashes, this makes a smash hit of a quilt. Quilt a pretty motif in each central octagon for a finishing touch.

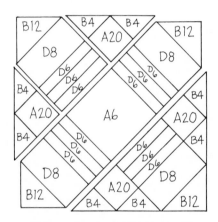

Children of Israel, 12″, pgs. 24 & 59

This simple, elegant block is at its best set straight with sashes or alternate blocks of rose. Press seam allowances on two opposite sides toward the center square, and press the other two seam allowances away from the center.

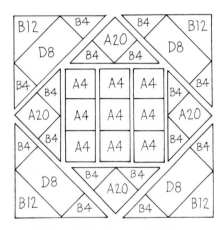

Hawkeye Block, 12″, pgs. 24 & 59

Set blocks diagonally with alternate squares of brown or black print. When joining blocks in diagonal rows, it helps to spread the blocks out on the floor and pick them up in order as you stitch them together.

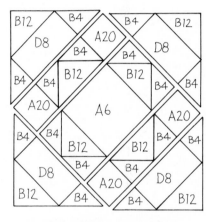

Monday's Child, 12″, pgs. 24 & 59

How pretty this block is set straight or diagonally with purple sashes or alternate blocks. Press seam allowances toward the cream background triangles.

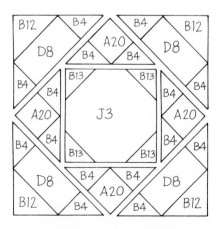

Surf's Up, 12″, pgs. 25 & 59

The distinctive wave print gives this block pizzazz. Set blocks straight or with alternate blocks. Be sure to press seam allowances away from the central octagon.

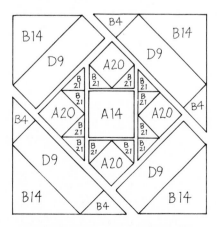

Baltimore Oriole, 12″, pgs. 25 & 59

For a striking, old-fashioned quilt, set Baltimore Oriole blocks straight with alternate plain squares. A border stripe adds a special touch to the rectangles.

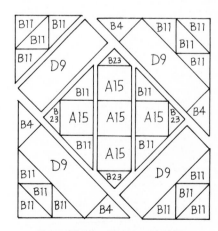

Emerald Isle, 12″, pgs. 25 & 59

Here is a fine block for someone of Irish ancestry or someone with an emerald birthstone. I like the block set straight with dark blue sashes. Press seam allowances away from the central Nine-Patch unit.

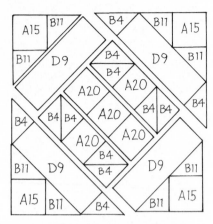

Baby's Breath, 12″, pgs. 25 & 59

Such a a dainty block for a new baby—or for a florist! Set blocks straight with pink alternate blocks or white print sashes. Press seam allowances away from the central Shoo-fly unit.

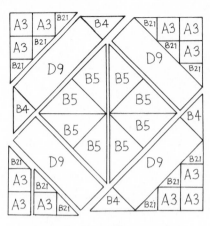

Setting Sail, 12″, pgs. 25 & 59

Blocks set with one-and-one-half-inch blue sashes and light blue setting squares make a jaunty quilt. The peach print has a faint stripe, which I cut so that the stripe would run the same direction throughout the block.

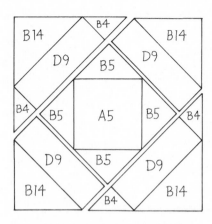

Boy's Nonsense, 12″, pgs. 25 & 59

For a quilt as lively as a little boy, set Boy's Nonsense blocks straight with navy alternate blocks. Press seam allowances away from the center square. For a special touch, cut the rectangles uniformly from striped fabric.

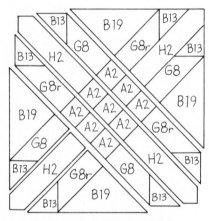

Mexican Star, 12″, pgs. 25 & 59

Who wouldn't enjoy taking a siesta under a quilt made from this lovely pattern? The block is traditionally set with adjacent blocks, but I also like it set straight with narrow sashes or with alternate blocks. Press seam allowances toward the H patches.

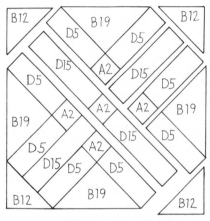

Denver Mint, 12″, pgs. 25 & 59

Set blocks straight with pink alternate blocks for a quilt as soft and sweet as a party mint. Choose two shades of one color plus contrasting accent and background colors for a pretty effect.

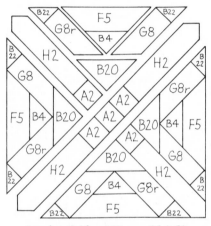

London Bridge, 12″, pgs. 25 & 59

I like this pattern with blocks set side by side or set straight with sashes. Be sure to have plenty of contrast between fabrics.

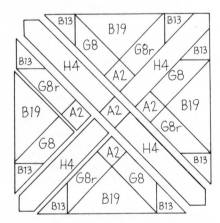

Star & Cross, 12″, pgs. 26 & 59

Set blocks straight with narrow sashes of pink or blue. Press seam allowances toward the blue striped patches.

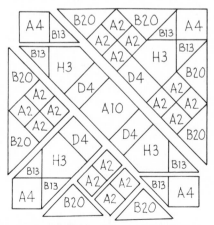

Country Boy, 12″, pgs. 26 & 60

Deep, dark colors and a rustic plaid give this block its boyish appeal. Set blocks straight with turkey red or navy plaid sashes two to three inches wide. The tea-colored muslin gives an antique patina to the background.

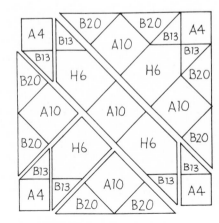

Springfield, 12″, pgs. 26 & 60

Set blocks straight with alternate blocks of the darker green for a fresh, springy look. Press seam allowances toward the background triangles and away from the arrow-shaped patches.

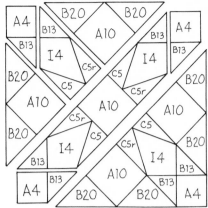

Song & Dance, 12″, pgs. 26 & 60

Blocks set straight with turquoise sashes make a lyrical composition. The three colors must contrast in order for the star to emerge. Press seam allowances toward the edge triangles.

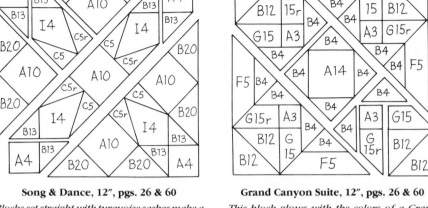

Grand Canyon Suite, 12″, pgs. 26 & 60

This block glows with the colors of a Grand Canyon sunset. For a magnificent quilt, sure to be an American classic, set blocks straight with dark pink sashes. Choose several shades of one color for a gently graded effect.

June Bride, 12″, pgs. 26 & 60

Set blocks straight with turquoise alternate blocks for a fresh, appealing quilt. In this case, I pressed all four seam allowances toward the center square for crisper points.

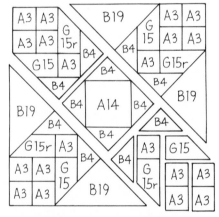

Auntie's Favorite, 12″, pgs. 26 & 60

Lilacs, roses, and the morning light filtered through lace curtains are some of the images this block brings to mind. For a lovely, feminine quilt, set the blocks straight, either side by side or with narrow pink sashes.

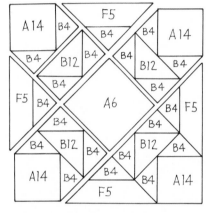

Valley of the Sun, 12″, pgs. 26 & 60

I don't usually change a block's existing name, but Snowball Stars seemed so totally inappropriate in this color scheme that I renamed my block here. Solid colors, carefully graded, add intensity. Set blocks straight with red sashes.

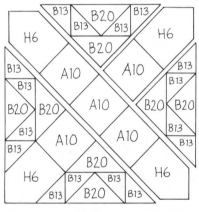

Swing in the Center, 12″, pgs. 26 & 60

Set blocks straight, side by side, varying the background fabric from block to block, or set blocks with black or rust sashes. Press seam allowances toward the arrow patches. Press the seams of the rust triangles away from the large white triangles.

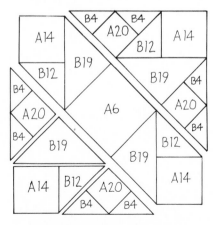

Home Grown, 12″, pgs. 26 & 60

A lovingly handmade quilt of Home Grown blocks set straight with navy sashes or brown alternate blocks would be a delight. Press seam allowances away from the corner squares and toward the edge triangles.

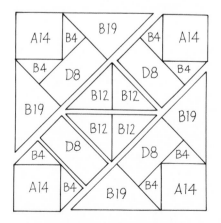

Octoberfest, 12″, pgs. 26 & 60

For a lively quilt with a fall feeling, set blocks straight with brown or rust sashing. Press seam allowances toward the rectangles' long edges, and press seams away from the corner squares.

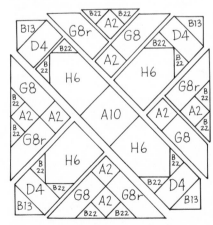

Chinatown, 12″, pgs. 26 & 60

Blocks set straight with alternate squares of gray or black make an exotic quilt. Be sure to cut the D and G patches from the same part of the stripe to achieve a twisted ribbon effect. Press seam allowances toward the stripe.

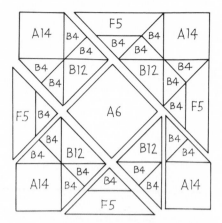

Georgetown Loop, 12″, pgs. 27 & 60

This is a variation of a traditional Georgetown Circles block. Set the blocks diagonally with navy or wine sashes for a striking quilt. Choose two close shades of one color for the star points.

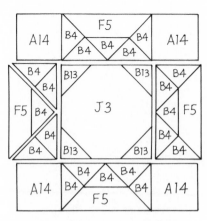

Sparks Flyin', 12″, pgs. 27 & 60

This block is similar to the Georgetown Loop pattern, but in just two fabrics it appears quite different. Set blocks diagonally with red sashes for an old-fashioned look. Quilt a pretty feathered circle or other motif in each octagon.

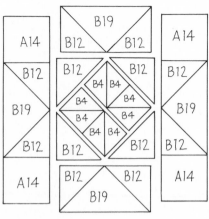

Martha Washington Star, 12″, pgs. 27 & 60

For a stately quilt, set blocks straight or diagonally with wine sashes and white or gray setting squares. Notice the way the stripes run in the white background fabric.

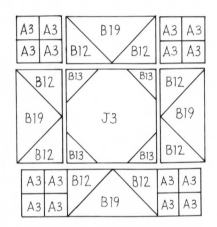

Taj Mahal, 12″, pgs. 27 & 60

Set blocks straight with one-and-one-half-inch white sashes and pink setting squares for an exotic effect of floating stars linked by chains of squares. Press seam allowances toward the octagon for crisp points.

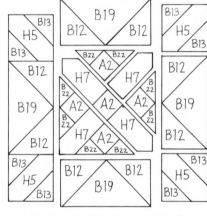

The Royal Mile, 12″, pgs. 27 & 60

In Edinburgh, the road leading up the hill to the castle is known as the Royal Mile. Blocks set straight with alternate plain squares would make a great quilt for a Scot. Press seam allowances toward the H patches.

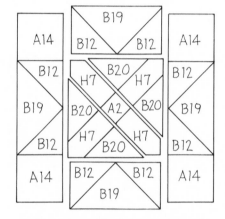

Independence Block, 12″, pgs. 27 & 60

Set blocks straight with three-inch sashes of red or navy for a delightfully old-fashioned quilt. Feel free to use a variety of scrap fabrics for added interest.

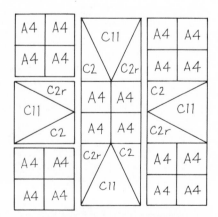

The Railroad Quilt, 12″, pgs. 27 & 60

More commonly known as 54-40 or Fight, I chose to use another, more friendly, of its names. Set the blocks straight with brown or turquoise sashes. Press all four seam allowances toward the center square.

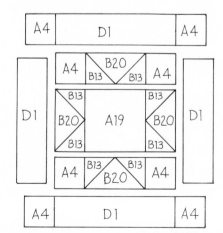

Green-Eyed Lady, 12″, pgs. 27 & 60

This simple pattern looks good in any set. Blocks set side by side can be of two different colorings for added interest.

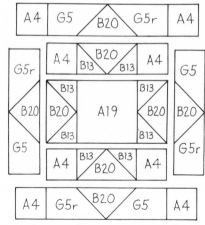

Hoosier Block, 12″, pgs. 27 & 60

Set straight or diagonally, with dark red sashes or light red alternate blocks, this is a handsome quilt. Press seam allowances away from the large triangles.

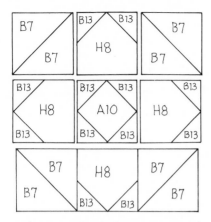

Smoky Mountain Block, 12″, pgs. 28 & 61

I like this block set diagonally with dark blue alternate blocks. Press seam allowances away from the center square.

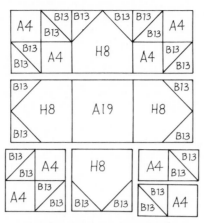

Weathervane, 12″, pgs. 28 & 61

A border print from Germany is perfectly suited to the arrow shapes and provides the color scheme for the block. A diagonal set with dark blue alternate blocks would be pretty. Notice how the background is darker than the star shape, an unusual effect.

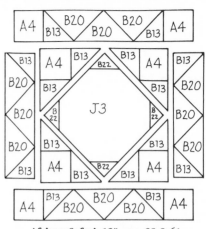

African Safari, 12″, pgs. 28 & 61

Serengeti colors set the scene here. A straight set with green alternate blocks would be attractive. Careful use of stripes in the tan patches gives a twisted-ribbon effect.

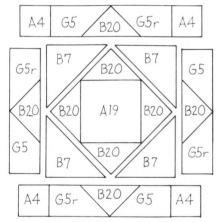

Cajun Spice, 12″, pgs. 28 & 61

For a zesty quilt, make blocks from different scrap fabrics and set them side by side on the diagonal. Press all seam allowances away from the center.

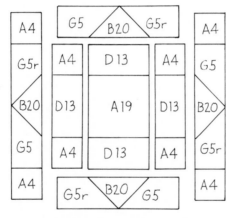

Oregon Trail, 12″, pgs. 28 & 61

Set blocks straight with medium green sashes for a pleasant quilt. I centered a floral print motif in each square. The quilt would also be appealing with blocks made from assorted scraps and set side by side.

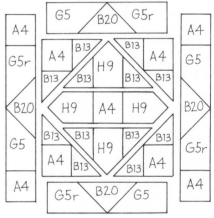

Grand Prix, 12″, pgs. 28 & 61

Here is a handsome block for the car buff in your life. Set Grand Prix blocks straight with two-inch navy sashes. The monochromatic color scheme of gradated blues and the careful use of stripes are noteworthy in this pattern.

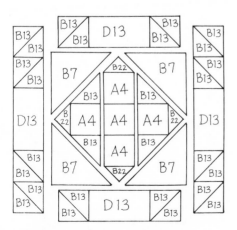

Florida Oranges, 12″, pgs. 28 & 61

Make a sunny quilt of Florida Oranges blocks set straight with orange sashes. Press the seam allowances of the green squares toward the white background triangles in the block center. Press the large triangles away from the center.

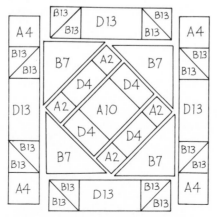

Prairie Nine-Patch, 12″, pgs. 28 & 61

Here is an interesting variation of a Nine-Patch. Set blocks straight with turkey red alternate blocks for an old-fashioned quilt. Press the seam allowances outward from the center of the block.

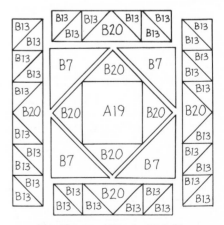

May Flowers, 12″, pgs. 28 & 61

Set blocks diagonally with purple sashes and light purple setting squares to make a quilt as fresh and sweet as a bouquet of spring blooms. Press seam allowances away from the center square.

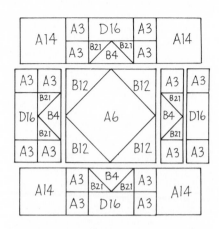

St. Lawrence Seaway, 12″, pgs. 28 & 61

This block gains its dynamism from the interesting use of stripes. Set blocks diagonally with medium blue sashes or alternate blocks. Observe the stripes rather than the grain arrows for the large and medium triangles.

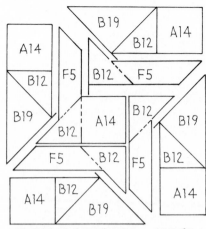

Daddy's Little Girl, 12″, pgs. 28 & 61

For a quilt that will be the apple of your eye, set blocks straight with two-and-one-half-inch sashes. Stripes add a special touch to this unique, layered-looking star. Partial seaming aids in the construction.

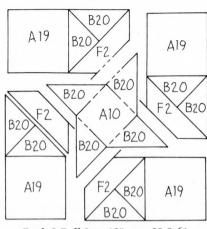

Rock & Roll Star, 12″, pgs. 28 & 61

The colors sing in this lively block. I like a straight set with blue sashes. Five partial seams are needed to make this block without set-in patches. Follow the diagram closely to avoid confusion.

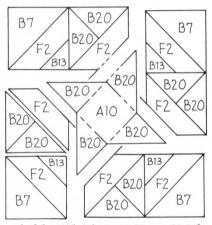

Land of the Midnight Sun, 12″, pgs. 29 & 61

This block has a haunting quality of light. Set blocks straight with blue sashing for a stunning quilt. The stripes seem to vibrate with energy. Notice the partial seams indicated on the diagram.

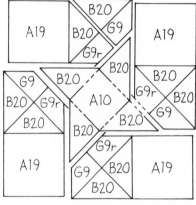

Black Forest Torte, 12″, pgs. 29 & 61

Chocolate brown and cherry pink make a surprisingly tasty color combination here. Set blocks straight with pink sashes for a scrumptious quilt. Partial seaming will help you make the block without any set-in patches.

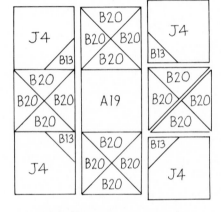

Baseball Star, 12″, pgs. 29 & 61

Set blocks straight with navy sashes to make a quilt that will please the baseball fan or player in your family. A monochromatic color scheme of gradated blues is effective here. Press seam allowances to oppose each other at joints.

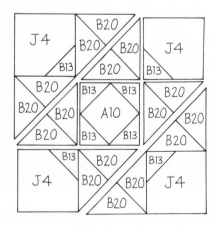

January Thaw, 12″, pgs. 29 & 61

This block is related to the Baseball Star, but it has a different center. Set blocks straight with pink sashes. Be sure to press seam allowances away from the center of the block.

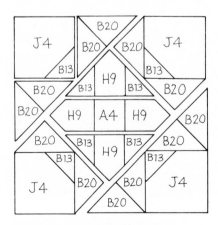

Golden Gate, 12″, pgs. 29 & 61

For a sunny quilt, set blocks straight with blue alternate blocks. The plain squares offer a golden opportunity for quilting a pretty motif. Scrap fabrics would add a colorful touch to the blocks.

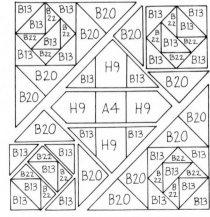

Vive la France, 12″, pgs. 29 & 61

For a most spirited quilt, set blocks straight with red sashes. Make blocks from scrap fabrics for a quaintly charming quilt, or make blocks from red, white, and blue solids for a strong, handsome effect.

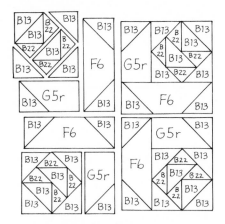

Guitar Picker, 12″, pgs. 29 & 61

Don't fret; this block is easier than it looks. Set blocks straight, side by side, or set them with teal sashes. Choose two shades of one color for the star points.

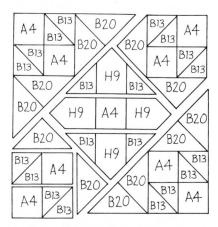

Carolina in the Morning, 12″, pgs. 29 & 61

This pretty block combines elements of a star, a Shoo-fly, and a Rabbit's Paw. For perfect points, press all four seam allowances toward the center Shoo-fly unit. Set blocks straight with teal sashes. Nothing could be finer.

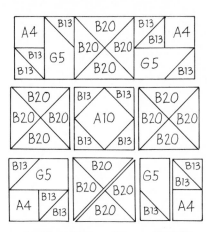

American Beauty, 12″, pgs. 29 & 62

Set blocks straight with deep wine sashes for an old-fashioned beauty of a quilt. Press seam allowances away from the center square-and-triangle unit.

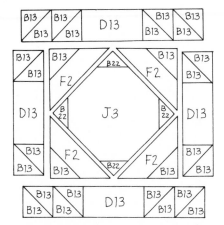

San Diego Sunshine, 12″, pgs. 29 & 62

Set blocks diagonally with rust sashes for a radiant quilt. Two shades of the same color are effective for the F2 and B22 patches. Choose a stripe for the F2 patches for definition.

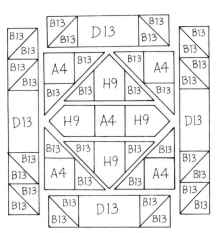

Truck Stop, 12″, pgs. 29 & 62

Set blocks straight with rust alternate blocks for a quilt with strong, masculine lines. A variety of scraps, including plenty of shirting plaids, would add interest.

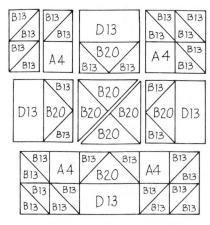

Spanish Moss, 12″, pgs. 29 & 62

Set blocks straight with green-and-rust striped sashes. The center "square" is actually four triangles cut carefully from striped fabric.

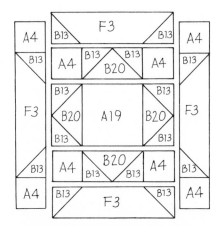

Cottage Garden, 12″, pgs. 30 & 62

Set blocks straight with blue sashes for a sweet quilt suitable for a gardener. I pressed all four seam allowances toward the center square. The seams that join the green to the white triangles are pressed toward the green.

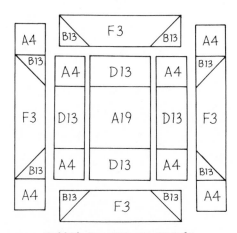

Rabbit's Paw, 12″, pgs. 30 & 62

Set blocks straight with two-inch sashes for a most traditional-looking quilt. This block is a favorite of the Indiana Amish. It is similar to a Bear's Paw, from which it probably derived its name.

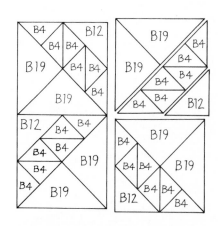

Happy-Go-Lucky, 12″, pgs. 30 & 62

Happy-Go-Lucky blocks set straight with green sashes make a carefree, totally delightful quilt. Observe the stripes rather than the grain arrows for the light triangles.

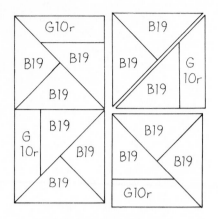

Pinwheel, 12″, pgs. 30 & 62

Here is a very simple quilt that is most appealing in scrap fabrics. Set blocks straight with navy sashes. Press seam allowances all the same direction so they will oppose perfectly for the final seam.

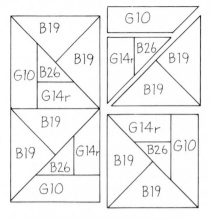

Shopping Spree, 12″, pgs. 30 & 62

This block is sure to please the "I love to shop" crowd. Set blocks diagonally with blue sashes, or make the quilt from vivid scrap fabrics for two completely different looks.

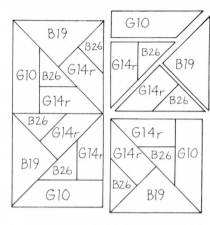

Kindred Spirits, 12″, pgs. 30 & 62

If you match the color of the stripe to the adjacent patch, a dual image of cogs and spinning pinwheels appears. Set blocks straight with black sashes for a handsome quilt.

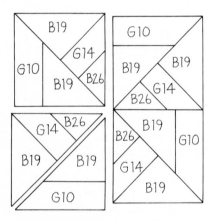

Mississippi Queen, 12″, pgs. 30 & 62

This pinwheel variation makes a quilt as graceful and old-fashioned as a Mississippi riverboat. Set blocks straight with pink sashes for a pretty accent. Press seam allowances all the same direction to oppose for the final seam.

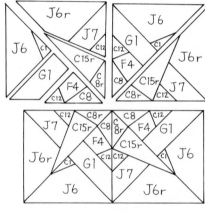

Mother's Day, 12″, pgs. 30 & 62

For a quilt any mother could love, join Mother's Day blocks in a straight set with red sashes or green alternate blocks. The block goes together effortlessly if you trim the points as indicated and press seam allowances to oppose at joints.

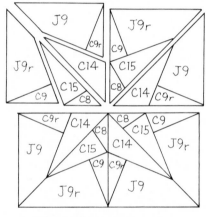

Manhattan Block, 12″, pgs. 30 & 62

For a sophisticated quilt, join Manhattan Blocks in a straight set with two-inch sashes of turkey red or black print. The block goes together easily if you press the seam allowances in each wedge to oppose the seams in the next wedge.

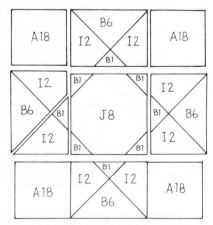

Peaceful Hours, 14″, pgs. 31 & 62

Peaceful Hours is a pleasant project to fill your spare moments. Make it with narrow blue sashes in a straight or diagonal set. Cut the small triangles from striped material, as shown, ignoring the grain arrows on the patch.

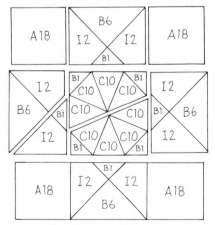

Enigma Star, 14″, pgs. 31 & 62

Isn't it curious that this block with eight wedges in the center can look so much like Peaceful Hours? The interesting effect is achieved by cutting all eight wedges out of the same part of a print. Set blocks diagonally with black sashes.

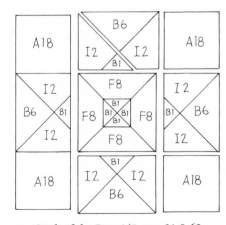

Catch of the Day, 14″, pgs. 31 & 62

This block is a prize when set diagonally with burgundy sashes. For an especially effective treatment, cut the F8 patches and center triangles with care from distinctive prints.

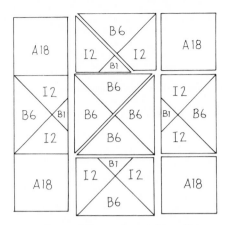

Old Dominion, 14″, pgs. 31 & 62

Made this way, Old Dominion looks very much like Twin Cities, at right. However, the center "square" here is actually four triangles cut from exactly the same portion of the same print. Red sashes and a diagonal set would suit this block.

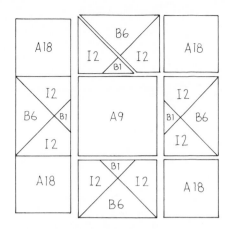

Twin Cities, 14″, pgs. 31 & 62

This simple star is pretty two ways: set straight with navy sashes or set diagonally with light blue alternate blocks. Either way, it goes together effortlessly.

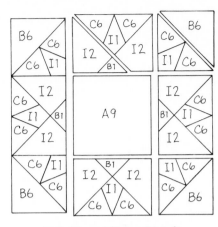

Early Riser, 14″, pgs. 31 & 62

Sunrise colors and a simplified Morning Star motif inspired this block. Set blocks straight with orange or blue sashes for an impressive quilt. Cut the C6 patches from folded fabric with the grain arrow aligned properly for the top patch.

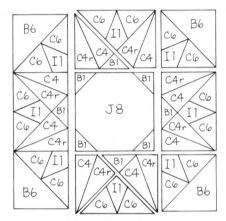

Vagabond, 14″, pgs. 31 & 62

Set blocks straight with teal alternate blocks or sashes for a sophisticated quilt. The block has the look of a Mariner's Compass, but without the tricky curves. Press seam allowances open along the seams joining C4 and C4r patches.

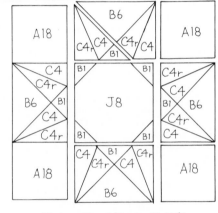

Kansas City, 14″, pgs. 31 & 63

Jazz up this simple block with a diagonal set accented by dark green sashes and light green setting squares. Press seam allowances open between C4 and C4r patches for perfectly smooth joints.

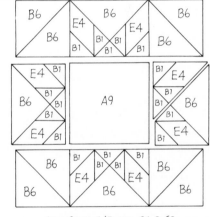

Amethyst, 14″, pgs. 31 & 63

Set straight with black print sashes, this makes a glorious quilt. Press the diamonds toward the small purple triangles, and press two sides away from and two sides toward the center square. Cut all of the large light purple triangles with the long edge on the straight grain.

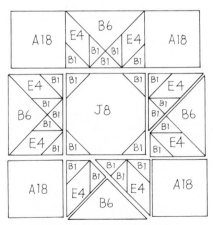

August Block, 14″, pgs. 31 & 63

August Blocks set diagonally with rust sashes would make a radiant quilt. Press the seam allowances that join the diamonds to the small, gold triangles toward the triangles.

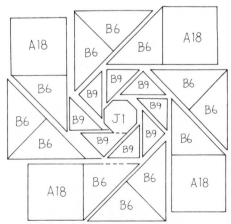

Building Block, 14″, pgs. 31 & 63

Set blocks straight with sashes for an attractive quilt. For the navy triangles, follow the stripes as shown here rather than following the grain arrows. Two partial seams permit you to make this quilt without set-in patches.

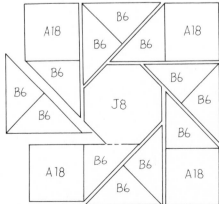

Waltzing Matilda, 14″, pgs. 31 & 63

This block is quite simple, thanks to partial seaming, yet its use of stripes is intriguing. A straight set with alternate blocks of rust is pretty here. Follow stripes as in the photo, rather than following the grain arrows on the patterns.

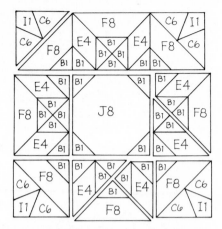

Dear Old Dad, 14″, pgs. 32 & 63

Set blocks straight or diagonally, side by side. An attractive secondary pattern develops where the blocks touch. For added interest, try alternating blocks of two colorings.

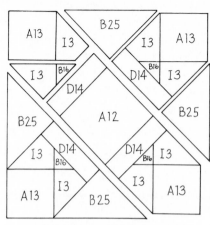

Union Block, 14″, pgs. 32 & 63

This block makes a striking quilt set straight with alternate blocks of rose. The rectangles were carefully positioned on striped fabric for an unusual, lacy effect.

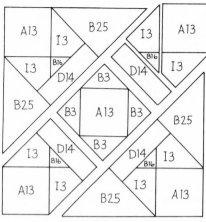

Tuesday's Child, 14″, pgs. 32 & 63

For a graceful, charming quilt, make blocks from a variety of scrap prints and set the blocks side by side or with sashes. Press seam allowances toward the background triangles and away from the background squares.

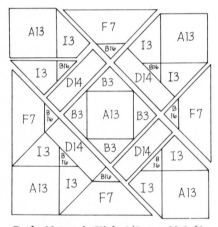

Rocky Mountain High, 14″, pgs. 32 & 63

Set blocks straight with rust or green sashes for a handsome, outdoorsy quilt.

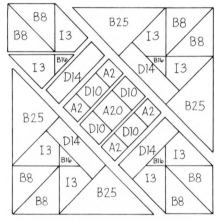

Baby Boomer, 14″, pgs. 32 & 63

Baby-soft colors set the tone for this delightful block. Join blocks in a straight set with sashes of the medium blue or with pink alternate blocks. A light border print was used in the background to frame the star.

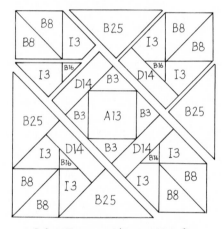

Orient Express, 14″, pgs. 32 & 63

Set the blocks straight with rich, red sashes for an elegant quilt reminiscent of a Persian rug. For this block, the A13 square was centered carefully on a floral motif and the background triangles were centered on a coordinating stripe.

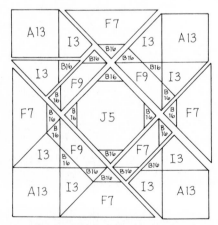

Viennese Waltz, 14″, pgs. 32 & 63

Set the blocks diagonally with sashes of the black stripe for a quilt with grace and style. Cut the B16 triangles with their short sides on the straight grain.

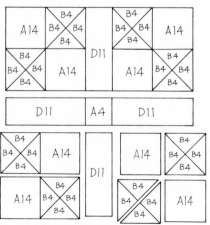

Celtic Block, 14″, pgs. 32 & 63

This block is pretty set straight with light green sashes. Be sure to observe the direction of the stripes, as shown in the photo. Cut the edge triangles with the long edge on the straight grain.

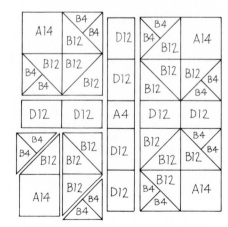

Southern Belle, 14″, pgs. 32 & 63

This feminine block looks sweet set straight with wide, lavender sashes. Cut the small triangles with the straight grain on the long edge.

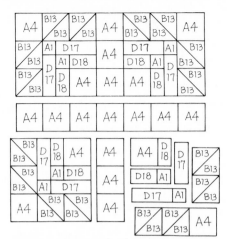

Patience Patchwork, 14″, pgs. 33 & 63

This is not a difficult block to sew, but it has many pieces and requires patience, as its name implies. Set blocks straight or diagonally with teal sashes for a glorious quilt. Two shades of the same color in the rectangles give a pleasant, shaded effect.

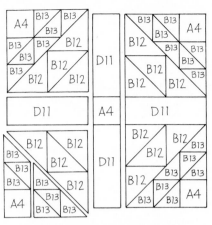

Whistling Dixie, 14″, pgs. 33 & 63

Crisp, masculine colors define this block. A straight set with burgundy sashes would be attractive here. Observe the stripe rather than grain arrows for the small, light triangles.

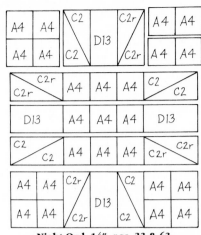

Night Owl, 14″, pgs. 33 & 63

Set these blocks straight with black or purple print sashes. Notice how the large print in the rectangles adds a contemporary flair to the block.

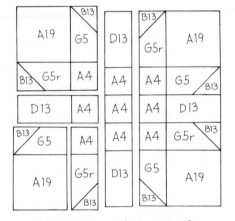

Girl Next Door, 14″, pgs. 33 & 63

Pink sashes and a diagonal set make a fresh, pretty quilt that is easy to sew. Make the blocks from a variety of scrap fabrics in spring colors if you want a more old-fashioned look.

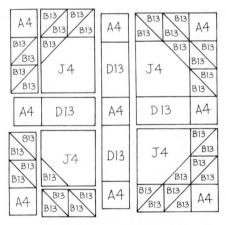

Ozark Beauty, 14″, pgs. 33 & 63

Set blocks straight with tan alternate blocks for a natural, handsome quilt. If you use a large print, such as the tan one here, consider placing each patch in the same position on the print.

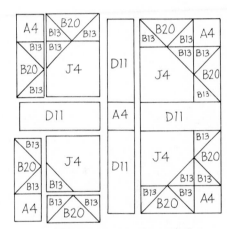

Texas Two-Step, 14″, pgs. 33 & 63

Bright, red sashes and a diagonal set make a rollicking quilt out of this cheerful block. The blue bandanna print gives the quilt block its western flavor. Cut the light background triangles with the long edge on the straight grain.

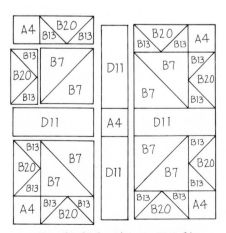

Fourth of July, 14″, pgs. 33 & 64

Navy blue alternate blocks and a diagonal set make a sparkling quilt with a patriotic theme. Cut the small, white triangles with the long edge on the straight grain.

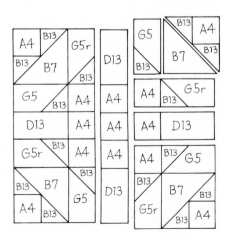

Sunny Side Up, 14″, pgs. 33 & 64

Set these cheery blocks straight with blue sashes and yellow setting squares for a quilt you'll love. I centered the printed motif in the four blue squares for a special touch. Press seam allowances away from the corner squares.

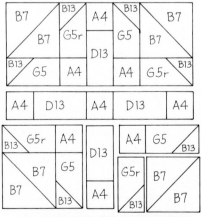

Puppy Dog Tails, 14″, pgs. 33 & 64

Here is the perfect block for dog lovers or boys (you know what the poem says that little boys are made of). Set blocks straight with two-inch brown sashes for a wonderful quilt to warm both heart and soul.

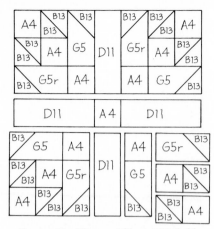

Brown-Eyed Susan, 14″, pgs. 33 & 64

For a quilt as bright and carefree as a summer blossom, set Brown-Eyed Susan blocks straight with two-inch turkey red sashes. Scrap fabrics would be an especially attractive choice.

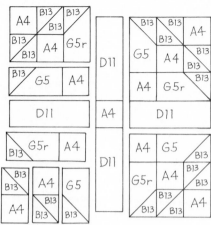

Gramp's Block, 14″, pgs. 33 & 64

Strong, dark colors give this block its rugged masculinity. Set the blocks straight or on the diagonal with turkey red alternate blocks to complete a handsome quilt.

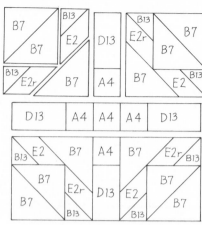

Puget Sound, 14″, pgs. 33 & 64

Puget Sound blocks make a handsome quilt set straight with two- or three-inch navy sashes. Center a printed motif in each of four squares for a special touch. Cut E2/E2r patches from folded fabric to yield the mirror-image pairs.

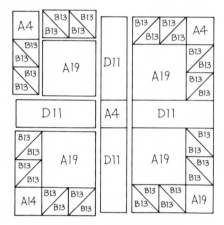

Bear's Foot, 14″, pgs. 34 & 64

This block is also called Bear's Paw. Set blocks straight with black print sashes and gold setting squares. For interest, be sure to mix the scales of the prints to include small, even prints, widely spaced motifs, and large, swirly ones.

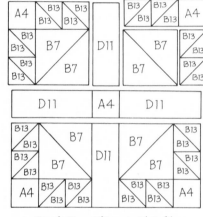

Bear's Paw, 14″, pgs. 34 & 64

This is a traditional variation of the Bear's Foot, shown at left. Set blocks with brown sashes or pink alternate blocks to make a cozy quilt that will take you from winter through spring.

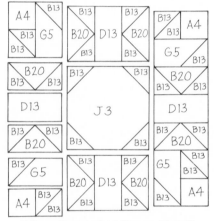

Calgary Stampede, 14″, pgs. 34 & 64

Set the blocks diagonally with turkey red alternate blocks for a handsome quilt. Be sure to cut the rhombuses one at a time, rather than layering the fabric, as no mirror images are needed.

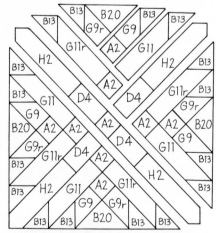

February's Finest, 14″, pgs. 34 & 64

For a quilt as fancy as an old-time valentine, choose February's Finest blocks set straight with narrow red sashes. Fabrics in three shades from red to pink should gradate evenly.

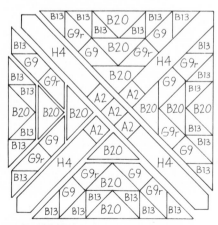

Norwegian Wood, 14″, pgs. 34 & 64

Set the blocks straight with brown or blue sashes for a lovely quilt. Cut the dark brown triangles and large blue triangles with the short sides on the straight grain. I centered the print in the small brown square.

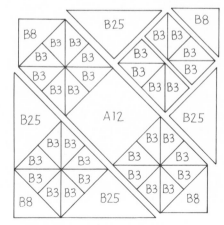

Merry Olde England, 14″, pgs. 34 & 64

For a jolly good quilt, set blocks straight with alternate plain squares of muslin, and quilt lavishly. Press two seam allowances toward and two away from the center square. Press all seams clockwise in the pinwheels.

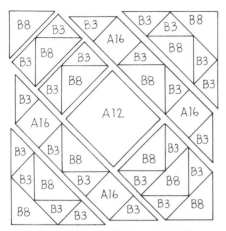

Ontario Lakes, 14″, pgs. 34 & 64

Sunshine and cloud shadows dapple the blue water of Canada's lake country. Set the blocks straight or diagonally with teal alternate blocks. The black adds a striking accent, eh?

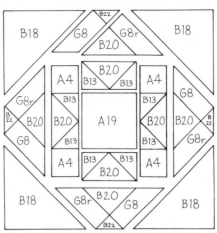

Collector's Block, 14″, pgs. 34 & 64

Here is a perfect quilt for the fabric lover. Collector's Blocks made from scraps of special fabrics and set straight, side by side, would make a lovely record of quilts that you have made or of prized fabrics in your collection.

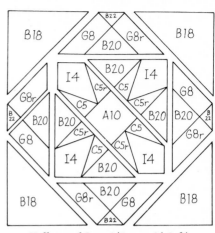

Hollywood Star, 14″, pgs. 34 & 64

Set blocks straight with sashes of blue or alternate blocks of the white print. Either way, the quilt is a crowd-pleaser. Press all four seam allowances toward the center square for perfect points.

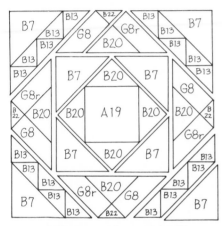

Taos Treasure, 14″, pgs. 34 & 64

Here is a block with a Southwestern air. Arrange blocks in a straight set, side by side or with narrow taupe sashes. Cut the dark teal triangles with their short edges on the straight grain.

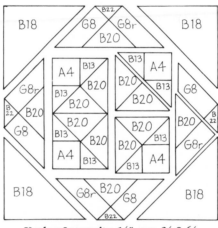

Yankee Ingenuity, 14″, pgs. 34 & 64

For an ingenious, double-pinwheel effect, make some blocks with dark blue corner triangles and others with light blue. Then, when you set the blocks straight, side by side, a secondary pattern develops. Cut the center triangles with the short edges on the straight grain.

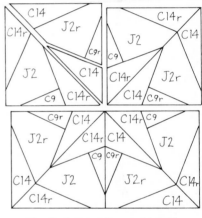

Teacher's Pet, 14″, pgs. 34 & 64

This pattern is destined to be a favorite. Set blocks straight, side by side, to create a secondary pattern of green four-pointed stars. Careful planning will help you oppose seams perfectly in neighboring wedges of the block.

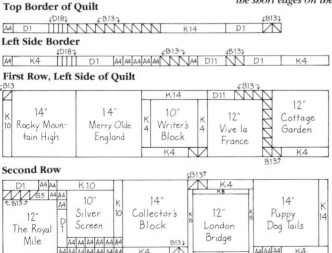

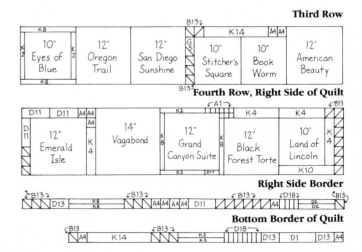

Personal History Quilt, 60″ x 74″, pg. 2

The rows run vertically in the quilt on page 2. The row diagrams here are "sideways." That is,

the top of the quilt photo corresponds to the right ends of the block rows as well as the two

longer side borders here. The top and bottom borders are as they appear in the photo.

QUILT BLOCK COLORING BOOK

This section features ready-to-color line drawings of all 174 quilt blocks. While each block is also shown in a color photograph, it occurred to me that you might want to do a little experimenting with colors of your own choosing. Perhaps you like the color scheme of one block and the pattern of another. By coloring the blank drawing with colored pencils, fine-point felt pens, or crayons, you can combine the elements that you like and see the results before you make the block. Feel free to photocopy the coloring book pages if you think you'll be wanting to color any block more than once.

You can also use the drawings in this section to help you plan quilts. Photocopy or trace the desired block or blocks and put them together in the set of your choice, with alternate plain blocks or sashes between them or just side by side. Photocopy the assemblage and color, if desired.

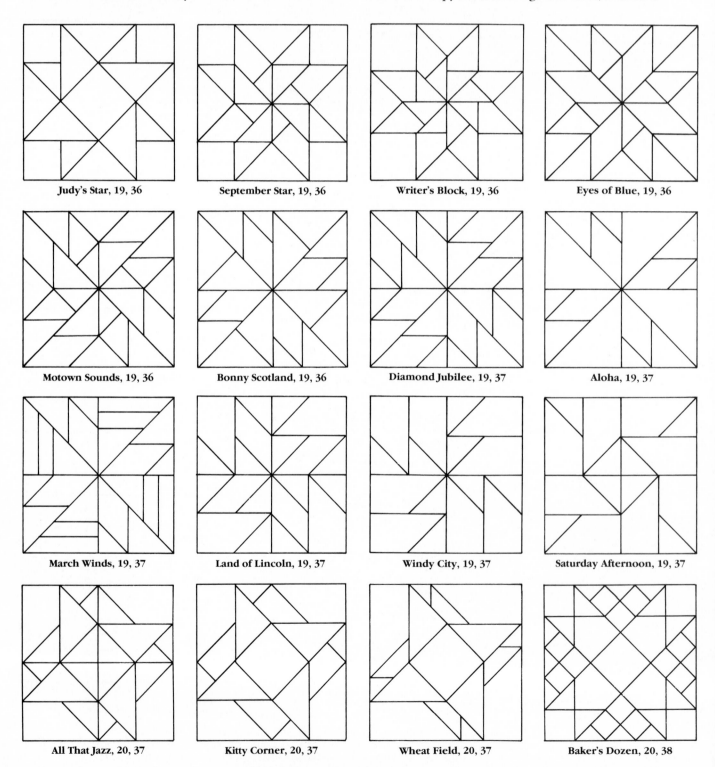

Judy's Star, 19, 36

September Star, 19, 36

Writer's Block, 19, 36

Eyes of Blue, 19, 36

Motown Sounds, 19, 36

Bonny Scotland, 19, 36

Diamond Jubilee, 19, 37

Aloha, 19, 37

March Winds, 19, 37

Land of Lincoln, 19, 37

Windy City, 19, 37

Saturday Afternoon, 19, 37

All That Jazz, 20, 37

Kitty Corner, 20, 37

Wheat Field, 20, 37

Baker's Dozen, 20, 38

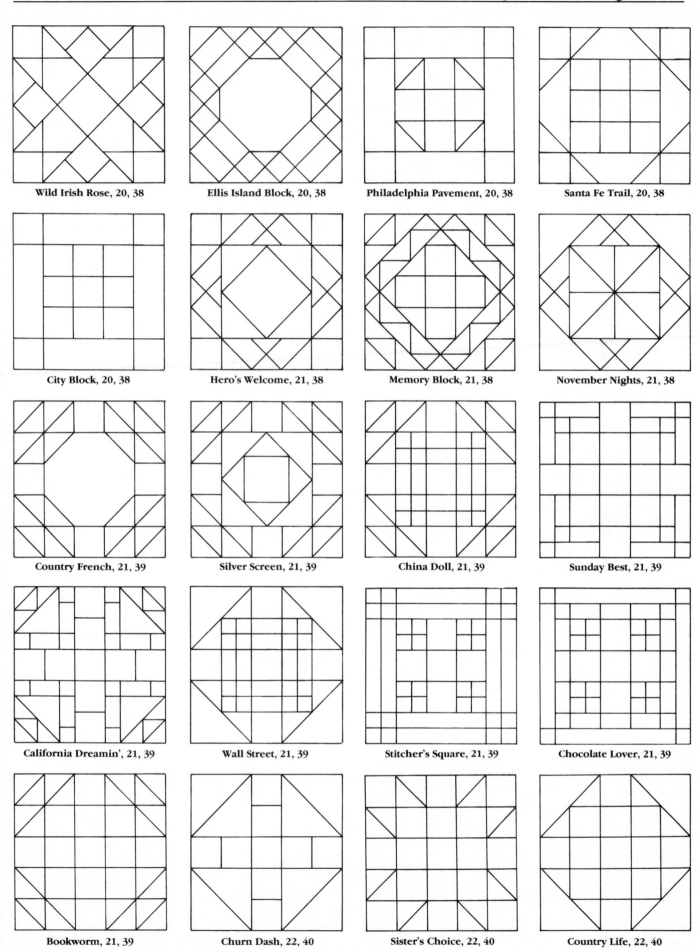

Wild Irish Rose, 20, 38

Ellis Island Block, 20, 38

Philadelphia Pavement, 20, 38

Santa Fe Trail, 20, 38

City Block, 20, 38

Hero's Welcome, 21, 38

Memory Block, 21, 38

November Nights, 21, 38

Country French, 21, 39

Silver Screen, 21, 39

China Doll, 21, 39

Sunday Best, 21, 39

California Dreamin', 21, 39

Wall Street, 21, 39

Stitcher's Square, 21, 39

Chocolate Lover, 21, 39

Bookworm, 21, 39

Churn Dash, 22, 40

Sister's Choice, 22, 40

Country Life, 22, 40

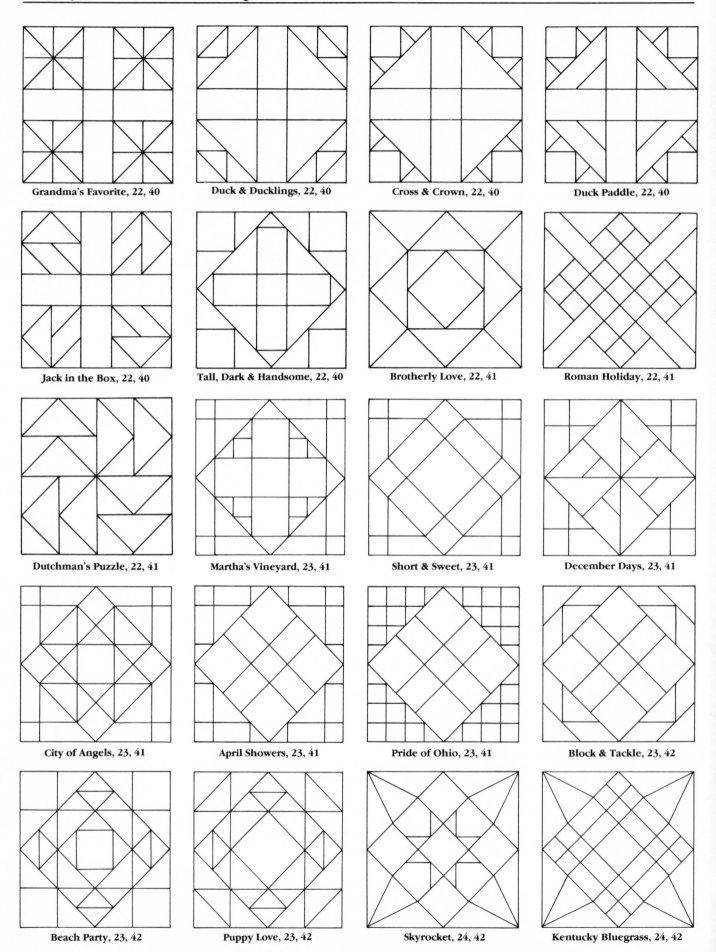

Grandma's Favorite, 22, 40

Duck & Ducklings, 22, 40

Cross & Crown, 22, 40

Duck Paddle, 22, 40

Jack in the Box, 22, 40

Tall, Dark & Handsome, 22, 40

Brotherly Love, 22, 41

Roman Holiday, 22, 41

Dutchman's Puzzle, 22, 41

Martha's Vineyard, 23, 41

Short & Sweet, 23, 41

December Days, 23, 41

City of Angels, 23, 41

April Showers, 23, 41

Pride of Ohio, 23, 41

Block & Tackle, 23, 42

Beach Party, 23, 42

Puppy Love, 23, 42

Skyrocket, 24, 42

Kentucky Bluegrass, 24, 42

Washington Monument, 24, 42

Georgia Peach, 24, 42

Star Sapphire, 24, 42

Royal Star Quilt, 24, 42

Roll On, Columbia, 24, 43

Kissin' Cousins, 24, 43

Broadway Nights, 24, 43

Children of Israel, 24, 43

Hawkeye Block, 24, 43

Monday's Child, 24, 43

Surf's Up, 25, 43

Baltimore Oriole, 25, 43

Emerald Isle, 25, 43

Baby's Breath, 25, 44

Setting Sail, 25, 44

Boy's Nonsense, 25, 44

Mexican Star, 25, 44

Denver Mint, 25, 44

London Bridge, 25, 44

Star & Cross, 26, 44

Country Boy, 26, 44

Springfield, 26, 44

Song & Dance, 26, 45

Grand Canyon Suite, 26, 45

June Bride, 26, 45

Auntie's Favorite, 26, 45

Valley of the Sun, 26, 45

Swing in the Center, 26, 45

Home Grown, 26, 45

Octoberfest, 26, 45

Chinatown, 26, 45

Georgetown Loop, 27, 46

Sparks Flyin', 27, 46

Martha Washington Star, 27, 46

Taj Mahal, 27, 46

The Royal Mile, 27, 46

Independence Block, 27, 46

The Railroad Quilt, 27, 46

Green-Eyed Lady, 27, 46

Hoosier Block, 27, 46

Smoky Mountain Block, 28, 47

Weathervane, 28, 47

African Safari, 28, 47

Cajun Spice, 28, 47

Oregon Trail, 28, 47

Grand Prix, 28, 47

Florida Oranges, 28, 47

Prairie Nine-Patch, 28, 47

May Flowers, 28, 47

St. Lawrence Seaway, 28, 48

Daddy's Little Girl, 28, 48

Rock & Roll Star, 28, 48

Land of the Midnight Sun, 29, 48

Black Forest Torte, 29, 48

Baseball Star, 29, 48

January Thaw, 29, 48

Golden Gate, 29, 48

Vive la France, 29, 48

Guitar Picker, 29, 49

Carolina in the Morning, 29, 49

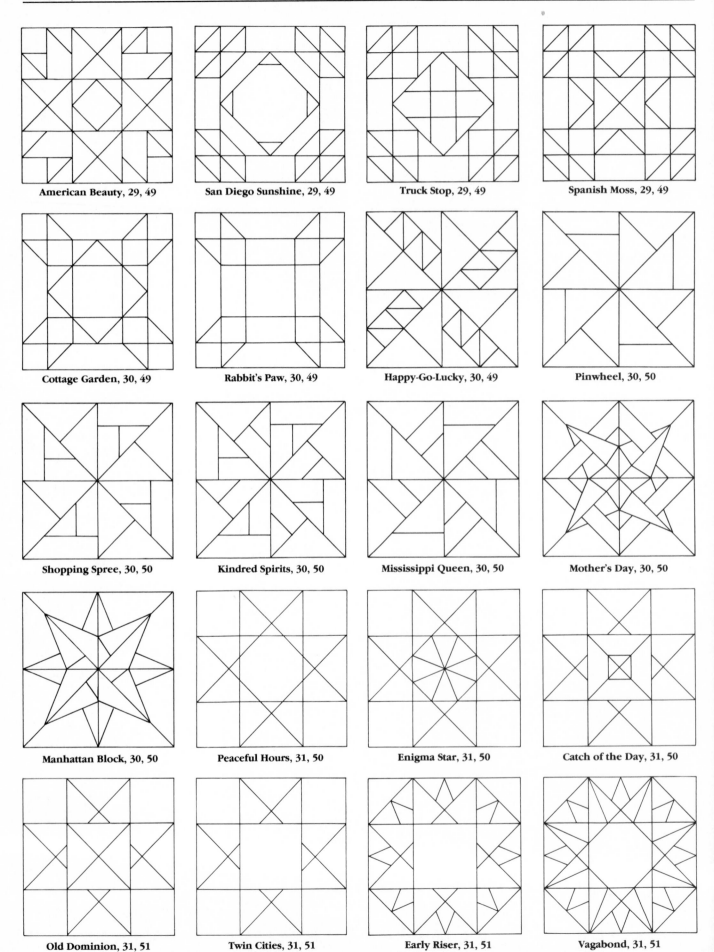

American Beauty, 29, 49

San Diego Sunshine, 29, 49

Truck Stop, 29, 49

Spanish Moss, 29, 49

Cottage Garden, 30, 49

Rabbit's Paw, 30, 49

Happy-Go-Lucky, 30, 49

Pinwheel, 30, 50

Shopping Spree, 30, 50

Kindred Spirits, 30, 50

Mississippi Queen, 30, 50

Mother's Day, 30, 50

Manhattan Block, 30, 50

Peaceful Hours, 31, 50

Enigma Star, 31, 50

Catch of the Day, 31, 50

Old Dominion, 31, 51

Twin Cities, 31, 51

Early Riser, 31, 51

Vagabond, 31, 51

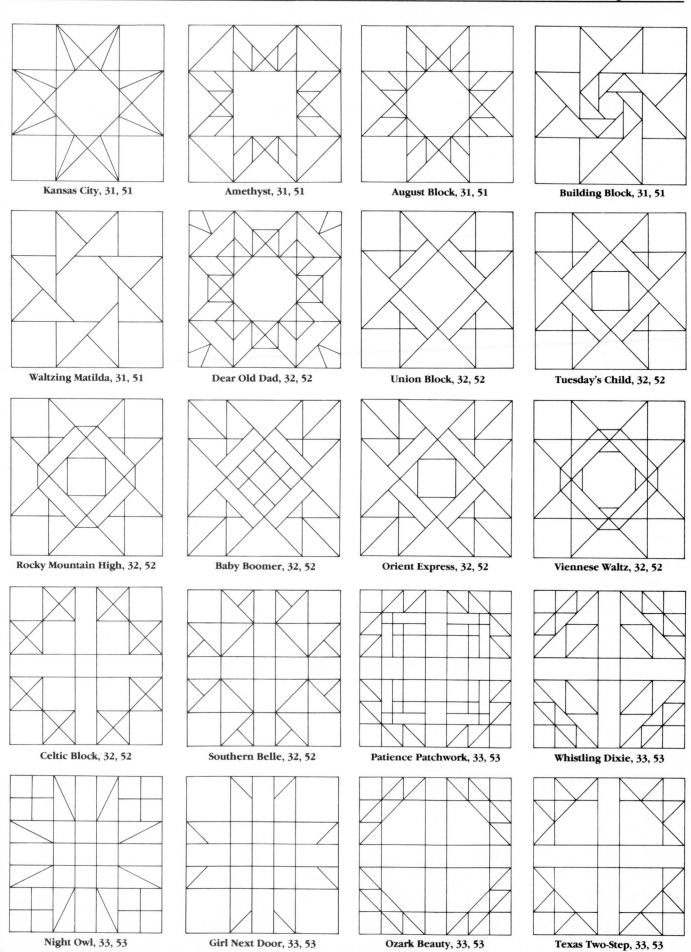

Kansas City, 31, 51

Amethyst, 31, 51

August Block, 31, 51

Building Block, 31, 51

Waltzing Matilda, 31, 51

Dear Old Dad, 32, 52

Union Block, 32, 52

Tuesday's Child, 32, 52

Rocky Mountain High, 32, 52

Baby Boomer, 32, 52

Orient Express, 32, 52

Viennese Waltz, 32, 52

Celtic Block, 32, 52

Southern Belle, 32, 52

Patience Patchwork, 33, 53

Whistling Dixie, 33, 53

Night Owl, 33, 53

Girl Next Door, 33, 53

Ozark Beauty, 33, 53

Texas Two-Step, 33, 53

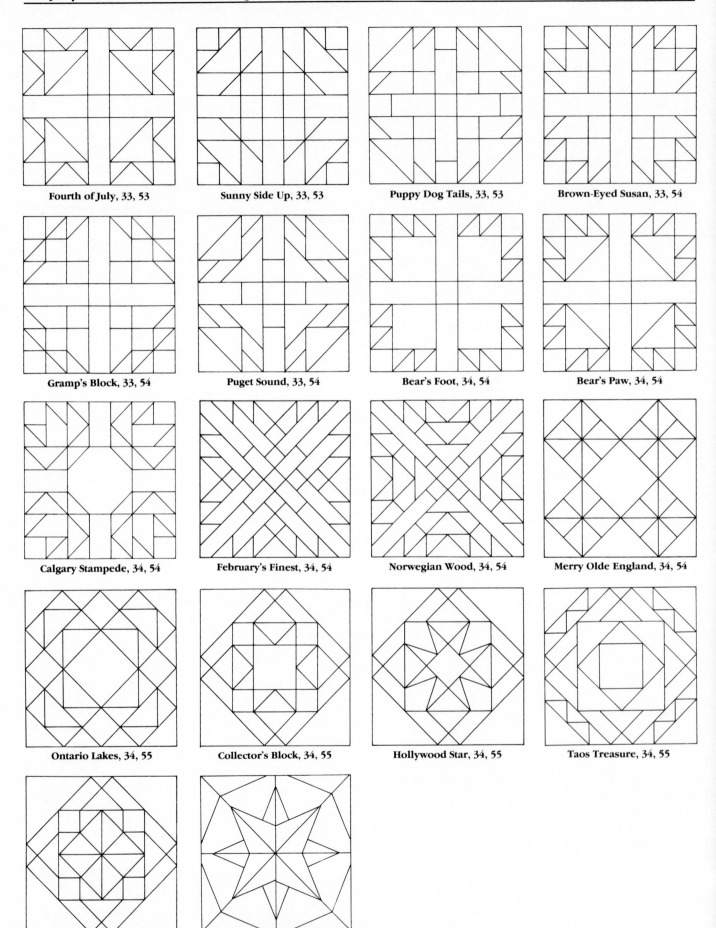

Fourth of July, 33, 53   **Sunny Side Up, 33, 53**   **Puppy Dog Tails, 33, 53**   **Brown-Eyed Susan, 33, 54**

Gramp's Block, 33, 54   **Puget Sound, 33, 54**   **Bear's Foot, 34, 54**   **Bear's Paw, 34, 54**

Calgary Stampede, 34, 54   **February's Finest, 34, 54**   **Norwegian Wood, 34, 54**   **Merry Olde England, 34, 54**

Ontario Lakes, 34, 55   **Collector's Block, 34, 55**   **Hollywood Star, 34, 55**   **Taos Treasure, 34, 55**

Yankee Ingenuity, 34, 55   **Teacher's Pet, 34, 55**

TIMESAVING CHARTS

HOW TO USE THE YARDAGE CHART

This section includes a yardage chart to tell you how many patches you can cut from one yard of 44"-wide fabric for every pattern piece given in the book. Each pattern is listed in alphabetical/numerical order. If your quilt plan calls for more or fewer patches than the listed number, divide your number by the chart number. This will tell you how many yards are needed.

For example, if you need to cut 124 A-17 squares, find A-17 in the chart; follow that line to the right to 99, the number you can cut from one yard. Divide 124 by 99. The result is 1.25. You will need to buy about 1¼ yards. Allow a little extra for insurance, buying 1⅜ yards instead.

If your quilt plan calls for fewer patches than the listed number, the procedure remains the same: If you need to cut 106 A-4 squares, look up A-4 on the chart. The chart indicates you can cut 224 patches from one yard. Divide your number, 106, by the chart's number, 224. The result is .47, which rounds up to .5. You will need to buy ½ yard or a little more, perhaps ⅝ yard, for insurance.

HOW TO USE THE QUILT DIMENSIONS CHARTS

This section also includes charts to tell you quilt dimensions for any block size in any of the six basic sets. Select the chart for your chosen set, straight or diagonal, with alternate plain squares, sashing, or adjacent blocks. Find the size of your block on the left. Follow that line to the right to the column headed by the number of blocks per row across your quilt. (Count blocks plus alternate blocks for this.) Where row and column meet, you will find the number of inches across the finished quilt, before borders. Repeat this procedure using the number of blocks down your quilt to find the lengthwise dimension.

Here is an example: If your quilt is set straight with alternate blocks, select the first quilt dimensions chart on page 66. Suppose your quilt plan calls for 12" blocks set in five rows of seven blocks each (18 pieced blocks alternated with 17 plain squares). Find 12" block size at the left. Follow that row right to the column for 5 blocks per row. Where row and column meet, you will find the crosswise dimension for your quilt, 60". Now, for the lengthwise dimension, follow the row for 12" blocks to the right to the column for 7 blocks per row. Your quilt will measure 84" in length, before borders.

YARDAGE CHART

number of patches that can be cut from 1 yard of 44″-width fabric

SQUARES		RIGHT TRIANGLES		OTHER TRIANGLES		RECTANGLES		MISC. PATCHES		MISC. PATCHES		SASH/ ALT. BLK.	
patch	*#/yd.*	*patch*	*#/yd.*	*patch*	*#/yd.*	*patch*	*#/yd.*	*patch*	*#/yd.*	*patch*	*#/yd.*	*patch*	*#/yd.*
A1	644	B1	416	C1	384	D1	64	E1	147	G14	126	K1	12
A2	378	B2	308	C2	112	D2	112	E2	112	G15	210	K2	84
A3	357	B3	221	C3	80	D3	140	E3	90	G16	147	K3	63
A4	224	B4	285	C4	126	D4	210	E4	126	H1	126	K4	48
A5	56	B5	154	C5	210	D5	154	E5	96	H2	105	K5	42
A6	56	B6	112	C6	144	D6	231	F1	200	H3	120	K6	36
A7	154	B7	112	C7	80	D7	144	F2	105	H4	84	K7	6
A8	120	B8	144	C8	280	D8	112	F3	64	H5	147	K8	56
A9	30	B9	240	C9	176	D9	80	F4	234	H6	84	K9	42
A10	120	B10	240	C10	132	D10	273	F5	105	H7	168	K10	32
A11	80	B11	286	C11	63	D11	80	F6	80	H8	63	K11	28
A12	42	B12	180	C12	420	D12	160	F7	56	H9	144	K12	24
A13	80	B13	336	C13	120	D13	112	F8	90	I1	208	K13	4
A14	120	B14	84	C14	90	D14	126	F9	126	I2	84	K14	32
A15	180	B15	374	C15	96	D15	105	G1	147	I3	104	K15	56
A16	154	B16	500			D16	210	G2	136	I4	99	K16	42
A17	99	B17	130			D17	280	G3	112	J1	154	K17	24
A18	63	B18	60			D18	392	G4	175	J2	45	K18	28
A19	63	B19	88					G5	112	J3	30		
A20	208	B20	192					G6	84	J4	63		
		B21	476					G7	70	J5	42		
		B22	500					G8	147	J6	65		
		B23	437					G9	210	J7	168		
		B24	198					G10	90	J8	30		
		B25	70					G11	105	J9	55		
		B26	240					G12	160				
		B27	70					G13	150				

QUILT DIMENSIONS

SOLID OR ALTERNATE BLOCK SETS, STRAIGHT

number of inches across or down the quilt, before borders
(includes both pieced and alternate plain blocks in number of blocks per row)

Block Size	Number of Blocks per Row (across and down separately)										
	2	3	4	5	6	7	8	9	10	11	12
10″	20	30	40	50	60	70	80	90	100	110	120
12″	24	36	48	60	72	84	96	108	120	—	—
14″	28	42	56	70	84	98	112	—	—	—	—

QUILT DIMENSIONS

SOLID OR ALTERNATE BLOCK SETS, DIAGONAL

number of inches across or down the quilt, before borders
(for width, count number of blocks with a corner touching top edge;
for length, count number of blocks with a corner touching one side)

Block Size	Number of Blocks per Row (across and down separately)						
	2	3	4	5	6	7	8
10″	28¼	42½	56½	70¾	84¾	99	113¼
12″	34	51	68	84¾	101¾	118¾	—
14″	39½	59½	79¼	99	118¾	—	—

QUILT DIMENSIONS
SASHED SETS, STRAIGHT
number of inches across or down the quilt, before borders
(includes sashes between blocks and around the edges)

Block Size	Sash Width	2	3	4	5	6	7	8	9	10
10″	1″	23	34	45	56	67	78	89	100	111
10	1½	24½	36	47½	59	70½	82	93½	105	116½
10	2	26	38	50	62	74	86	98	110	—
10	2½	27½	40	52½	65	77½	90	102½	115	—
10	3	29	42	55	68	81	94	107	120	—
12″	1″	27	40	53	66	79	92	105	118	—
12	1½	28½	42	55½	69	82½	96	109½	—	—
12	2	30	44	58	72	86	100	114	—	—
12	2½	31½	46	60½	75	89½	104	118½	—	—
12	3	33	48	63	78	93	108	—	—	—
14″	1″	31	46	61	76	91	106	—	—	—
14	1½	32½	48	63½	79	94½	110	—	—	—
14	2	34	50	66	82	98	114	—	—	—
14	2½	35½	52	68½	85	101½	118	—	—	—
14	3	37	54	71	88	105	—	—	—	—

QUILT DIMENSIONS
SASHED SETS, DIAGONAL
number of inches across or down the quilt, before borders
(includes sashes between blocks and around the edges, count each block with a corner touching the quilt edge.)

Block Size	Sash Width	2	3	4	5	6	7
10″	1″	31	46¾	62¼	77¾	93¼	109
10	1½	32½	48¾	65	81¼	97½	113¾
10	2	34	51	68	84¾	101¾	118¾
10	2½	35¼	53	70¾	88½	106	123¾
10	3	36¾	55¼	73½	92	110¼	—
12″	1″	36¾	55¼	73½	92	110¼	—
12	1½	38¼	57¼	76¼	95½	114½	—
12	2	39½	59½	79¼	99	118¾	—
12	2½	41	61½	82	102½	—	—
12	3	42½	63¾	84¾	106	—	—
14″	1″	42½	63¾	84¾	106	—	—
14	1½	43¾	65¾	87¾	109½	—	—
14	2	45¼	68	90½	113¼	—	—
14	2½	46¾	70	93¼	116¾	—	—
14	3	48	72	96¼	120¼	—	—

HELPFUL FORMULAS
FOR DETERMINING NUMBERS OF BLOCKS, SASHES, SETTING SQUARES, & ALTERNATE BLOCKS REQUIRED

You can simply count blocks and other patches, or you can use a little simple arithmetic to determine your quilt's requirements more quickly. For those of you who are comfortable with math, here are some formulas that you may find helpful. If this looks like gibberish to you, don't worry about it. Skip this section and figure your quilt's requirements as you always have.

For each of these formulas, L equals the number of blocks per row down the length of the quilt. W equals the number of blocks per row across the width of the quilt. To count blocks per row for alternate block quilts, count both pieced blocks and plain blocks. To count blocks per row for sashed quilts, count blocks only, not sashes. To count blocks per row for diagonal sets, don't count blocks in diagonal rows as you would sew the quilt. Instead, count the number of blocks whose points touch the top edge of the quilt (W) or the number of blocks whose points touch one side of the quilt (L).

Number of Blocks Needed

Straight set, side by side or with sashes:
$$L \times W = \# \text{ blocks}$$

Straight set, alternate blocks:
$$(L \times W) \div 2 \text{ (rounded up to nearest whole number)} = \# \text{ blocks}$$

Diagonal set, side by side or with sashes:
$$(L \times W) + [(L - 1) \times (W - 1)] = \# \text{ blocks}$$

Diagonal set, alternate blocks:
$$L \times W = \# \text{ blocks}$$

Number of Alternate Plain Blocks Needed

Straight set:
$$(L \times W) \div 2 \text{ (rounded down to nearest whole number)} = \# \text{ alternate plain blocks}$$

Diagonal set:
$$(L - 1) \times (W - 1) = \# \text{ alternate plain blocks}$$

Number of Setting Squares Needed

Straight set:
$$(L + 1) \times (W + 1) = \# \text{ setting squares}$$

Diagonal set:
$$[L \times (W + 1)] + [W \times (L + 1)] = \# \text{ setting squares}$$

Number of Sashes Needed

All sets:
$$(\# \text{ blocks} + \# \text{ setting squares}) - 1 = \# \text{ sashes}$$

FULL-SIZE PATTERNS

This section includes full-size patterns for all 174 blocks. Each patch has seam lines (dashed), cutting lines (solid), and grain arrows. The sash and alternate block patches were too large to fit on the page; for these, half or quarter patterns were given, with dotted lines indicating the halfway fold. Do not place these on the fold of the *fabric*. Instead, place them on the fold of a large piece of paper, and use the completed paper pattern to cut the fabric.

The patterns are organized by shape, with each shape designated by a different letter. Within a shape, different sized patches are identified by different numbers. Patches are in alphabetical and numerical order so that you can find whichever ones you desire quickly and easily.

Most blocks call for patches to be cut with the grain indicated by the arrow. Occasionally, a pattern may be used in different blocks with the grain running different directions in each. In these cases, two grain arrows are given. Choose the grain arrow that puts the straight grain on the outside edges of the block.

Quilting motifs are given for the larger sash and alternate block patterns. These are presented with dashed lines well within the seam lines of the patch.

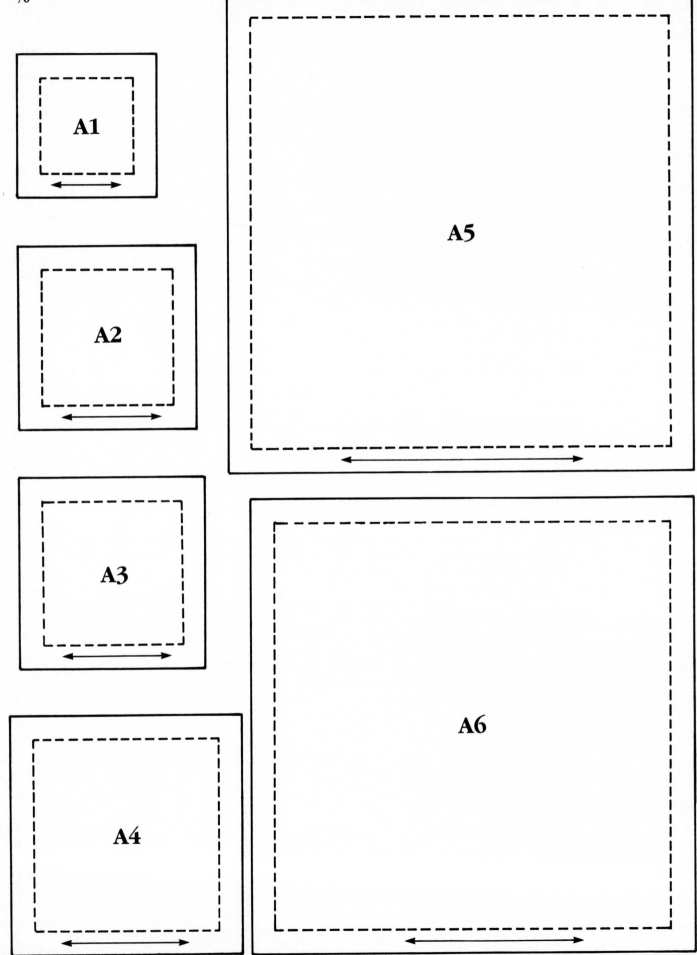

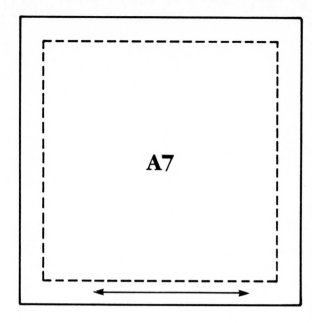

A7

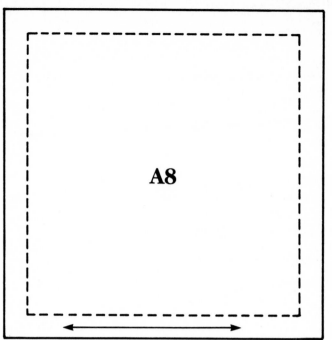

A8

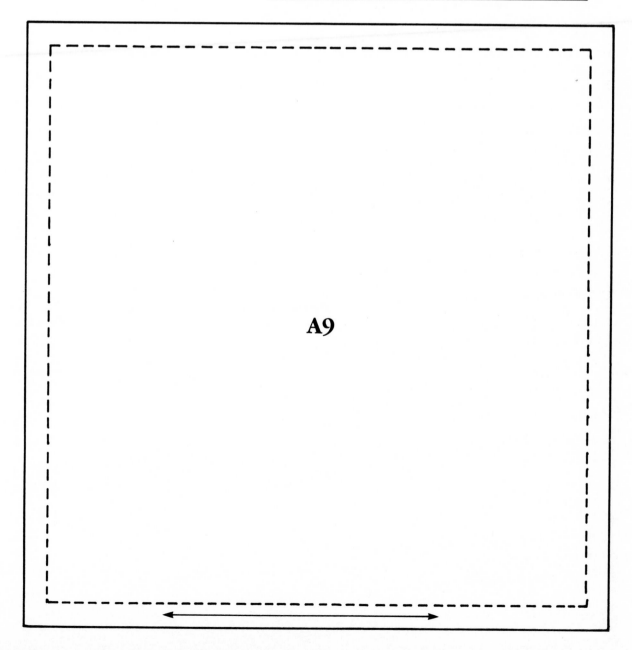

A9

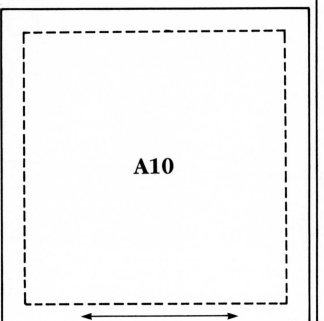

A10

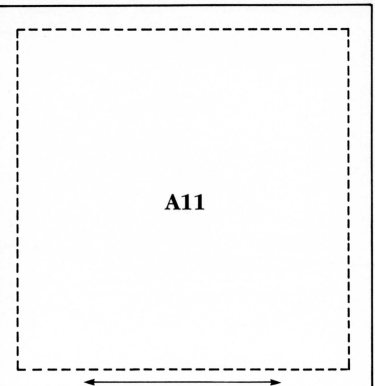

A11

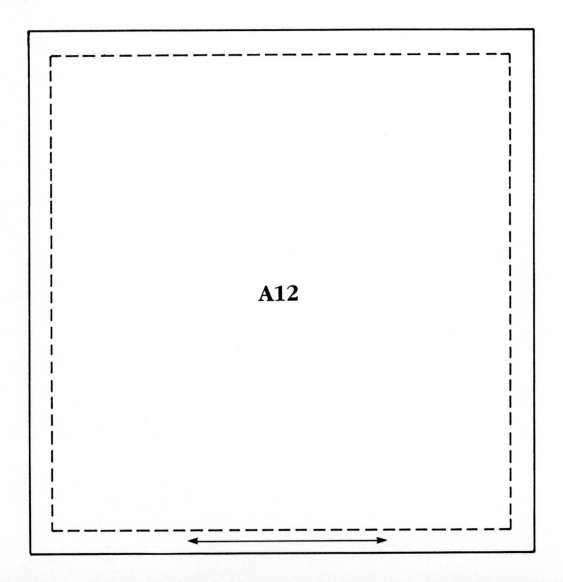

A12

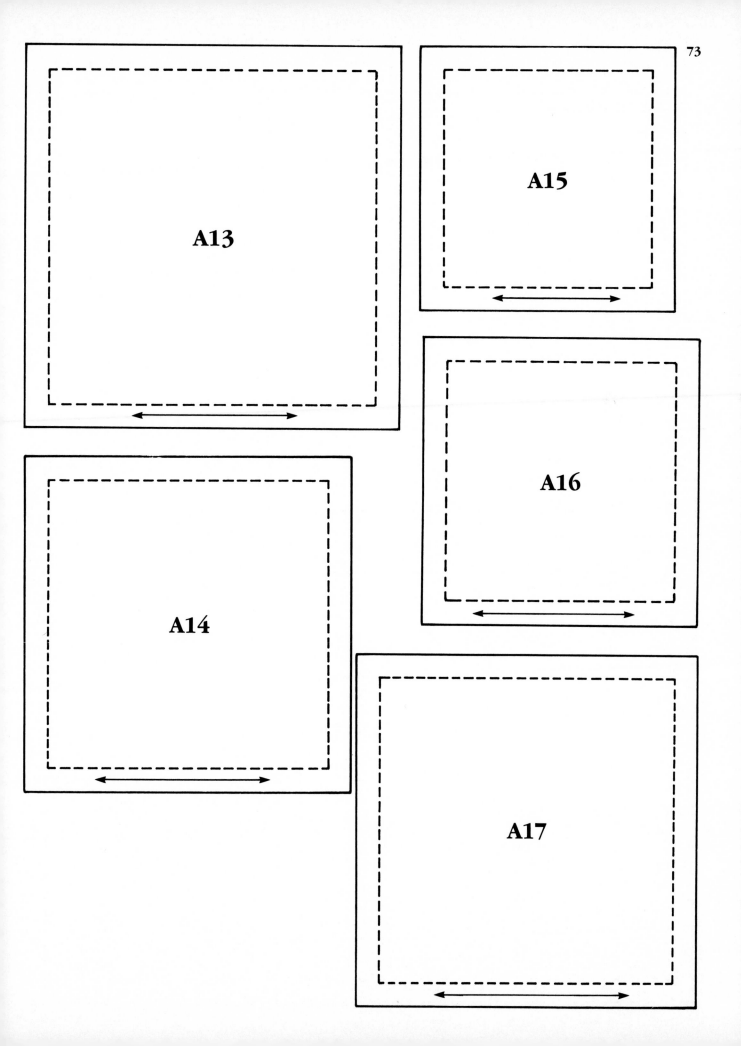

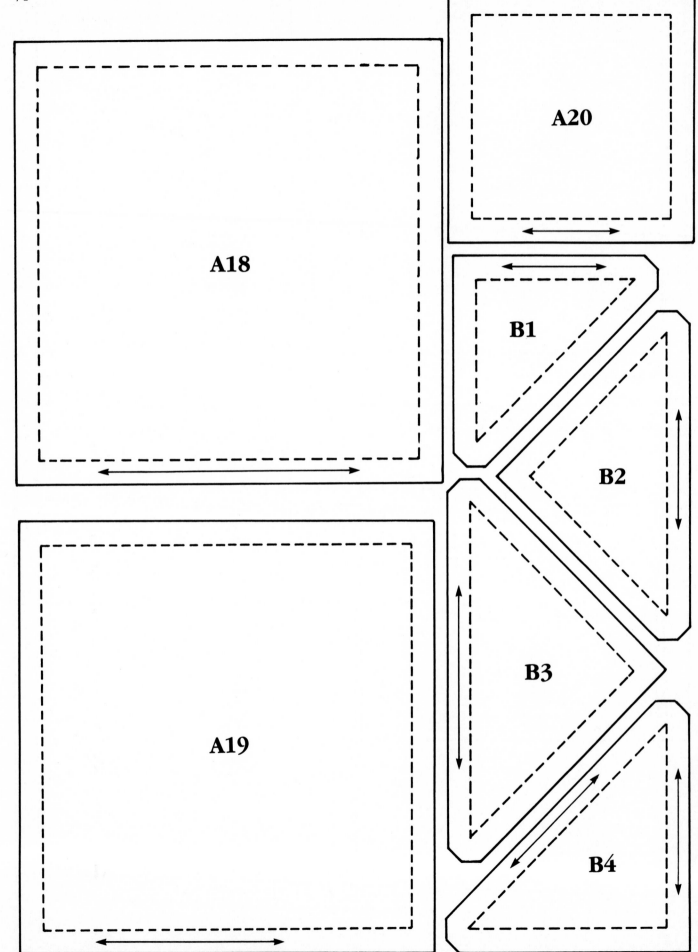

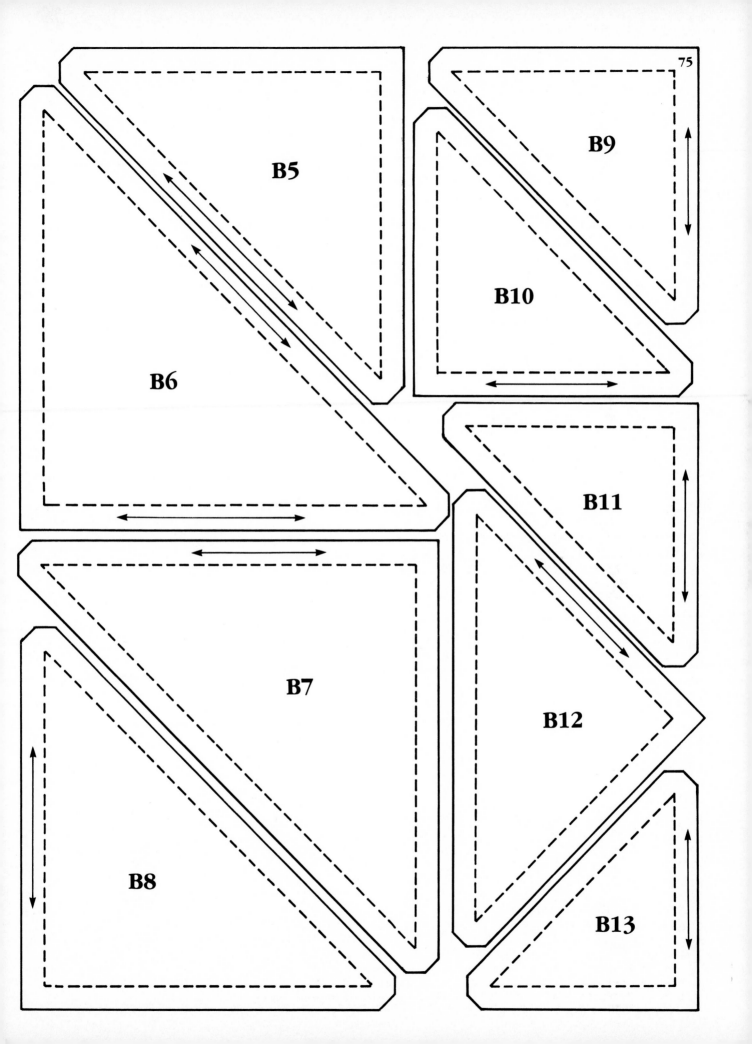

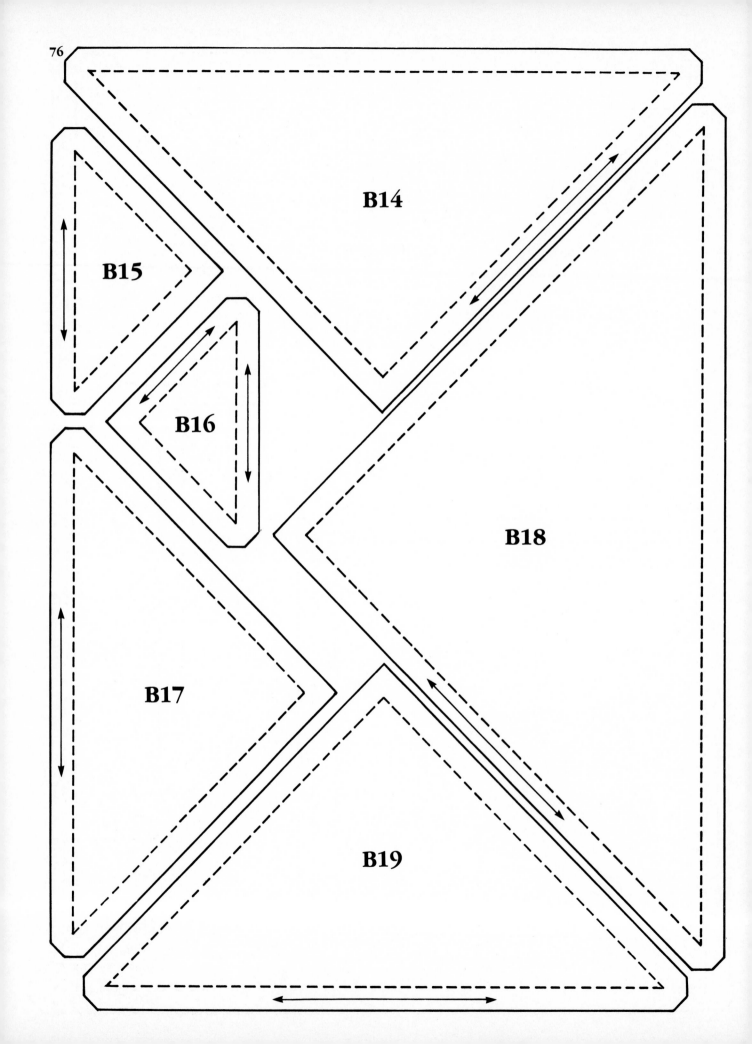

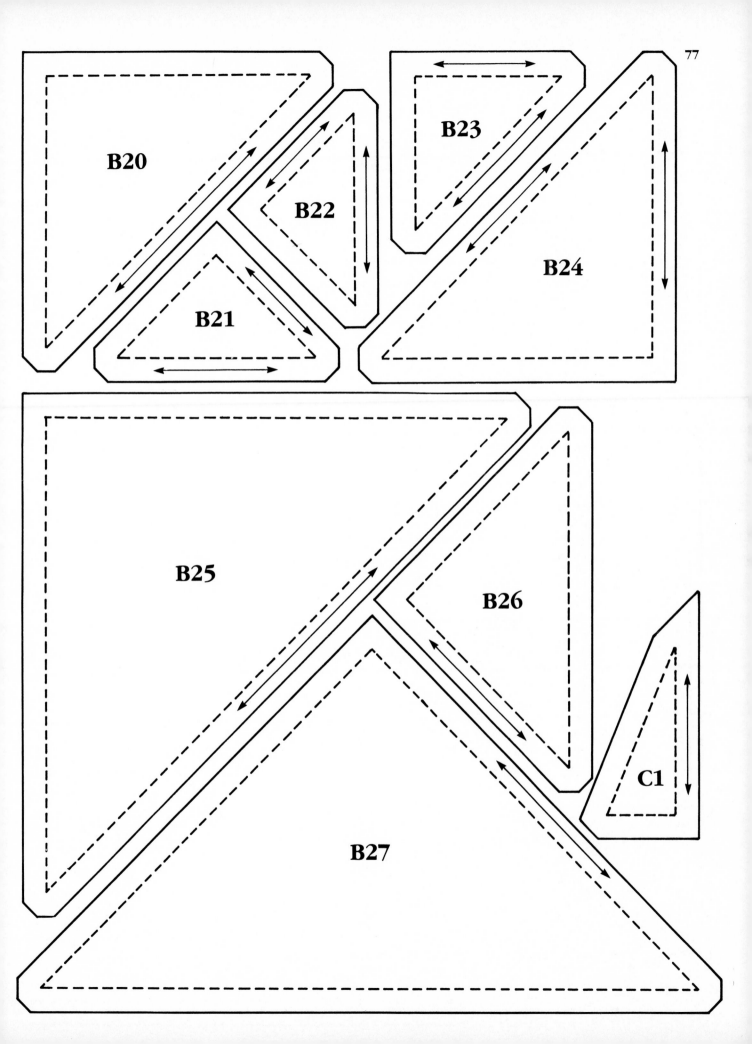

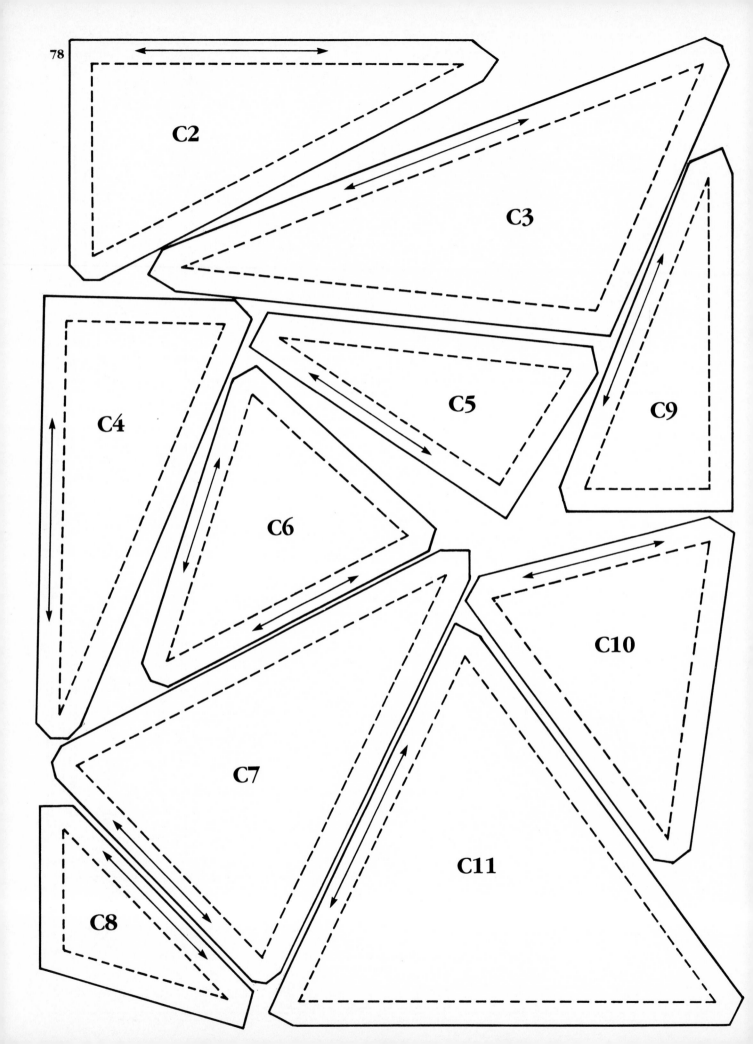

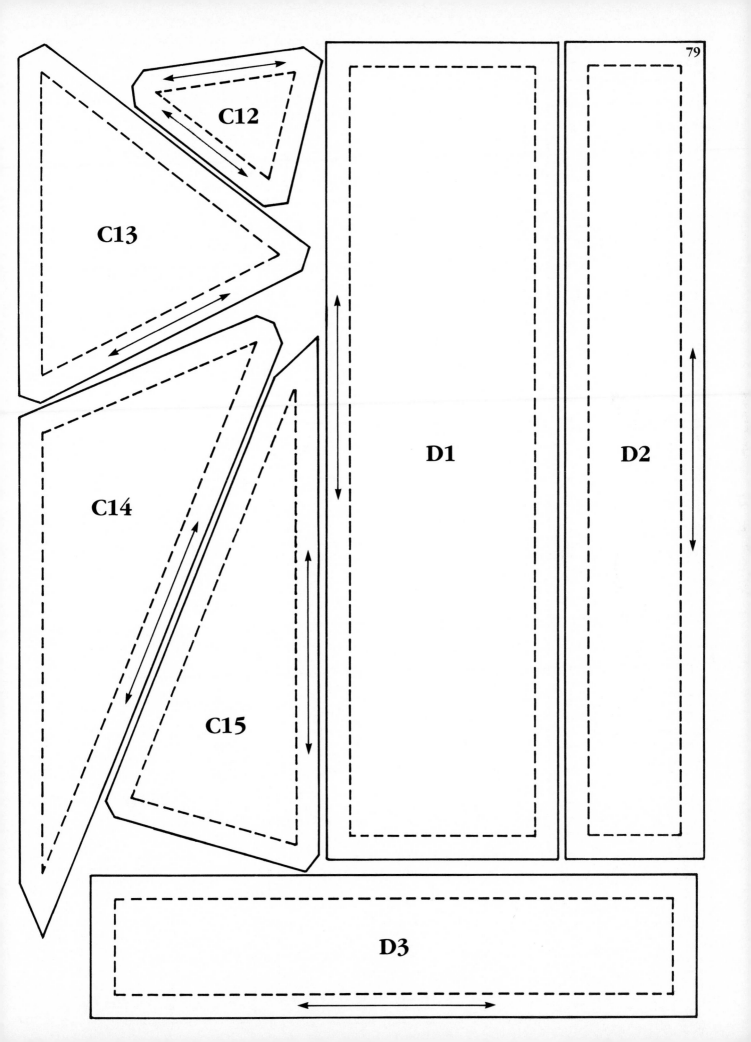

D4

D7

D9

D5

D8

D10

D6

81

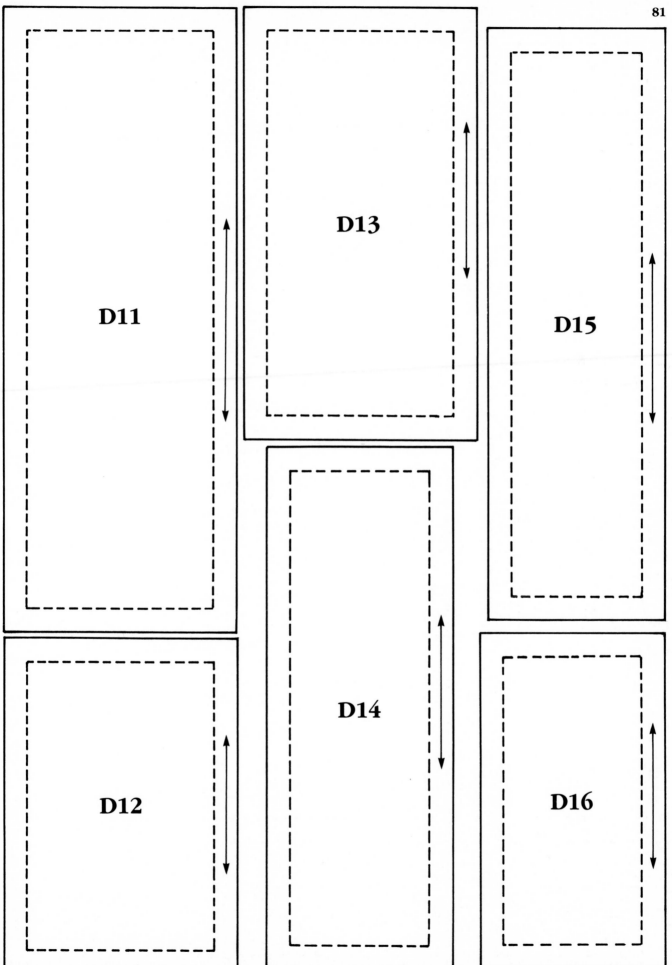

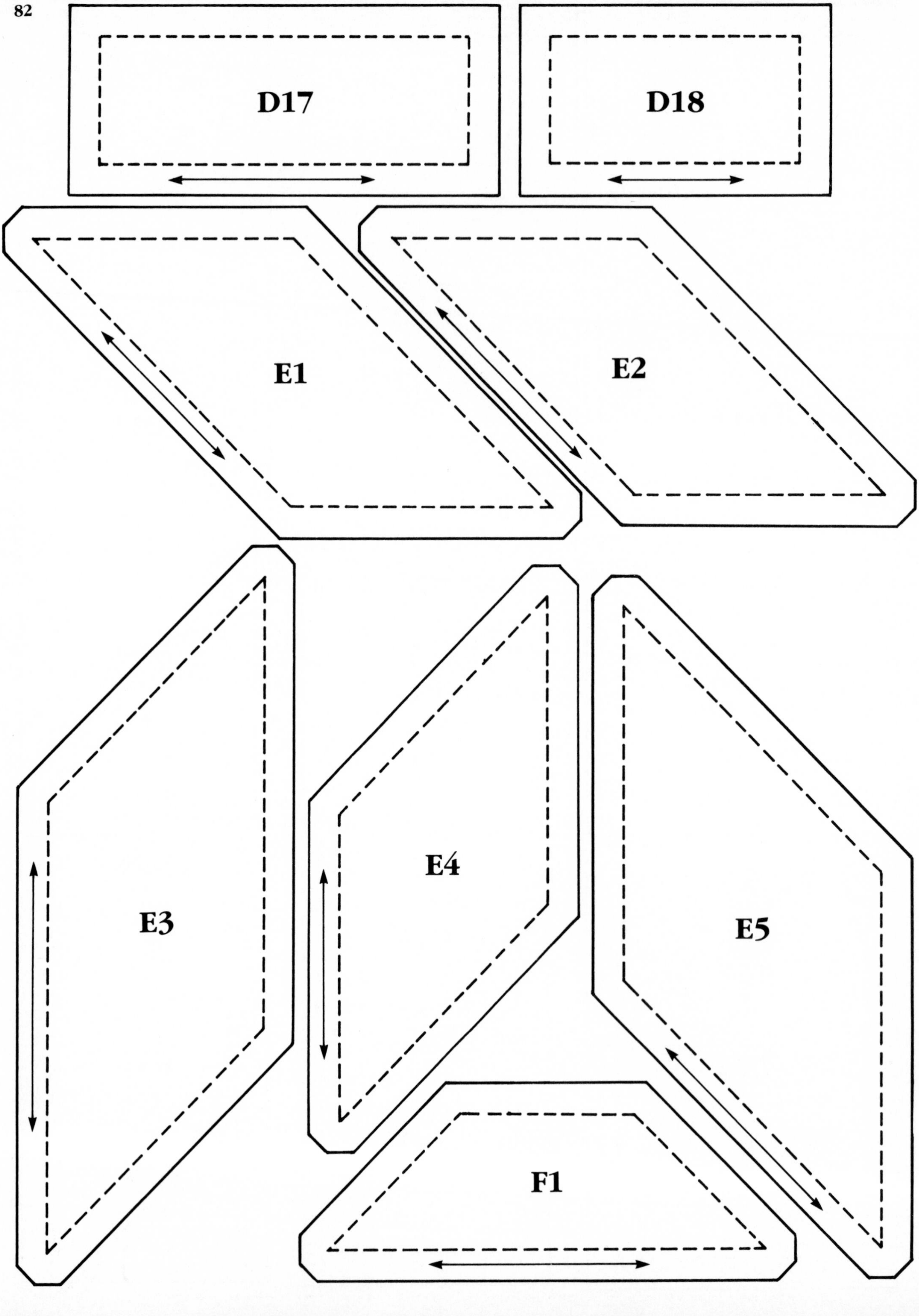

D17

D18

E1

E2

E3

E4

E5

F1

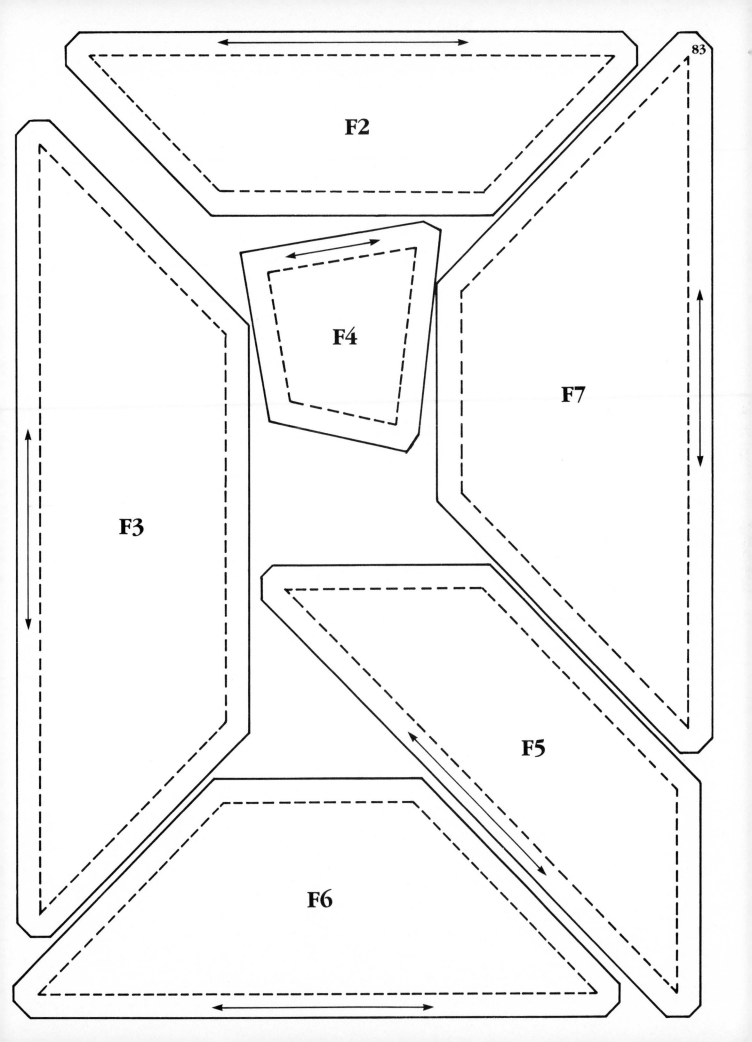

F8

F9

G1

G2

G3

G4

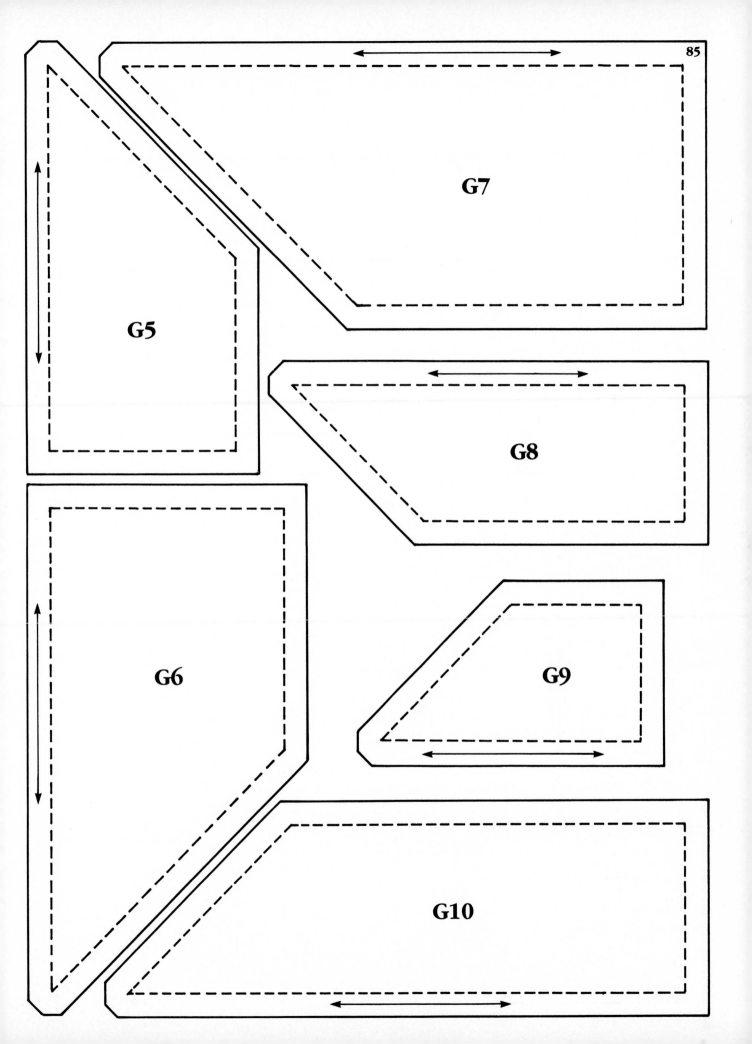

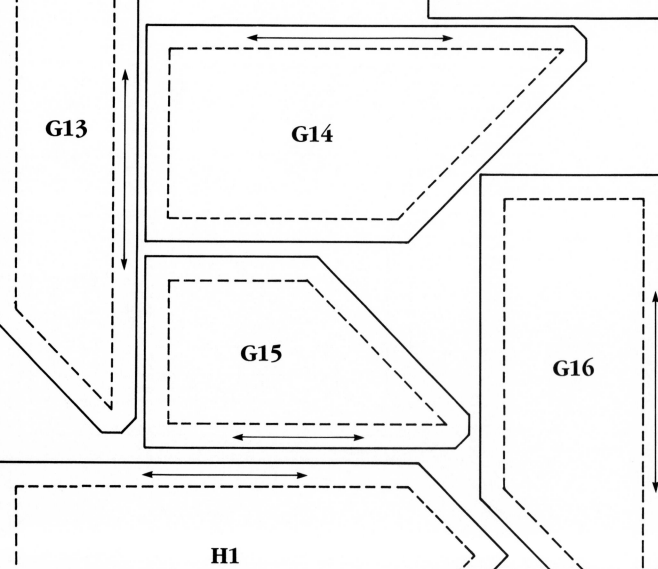

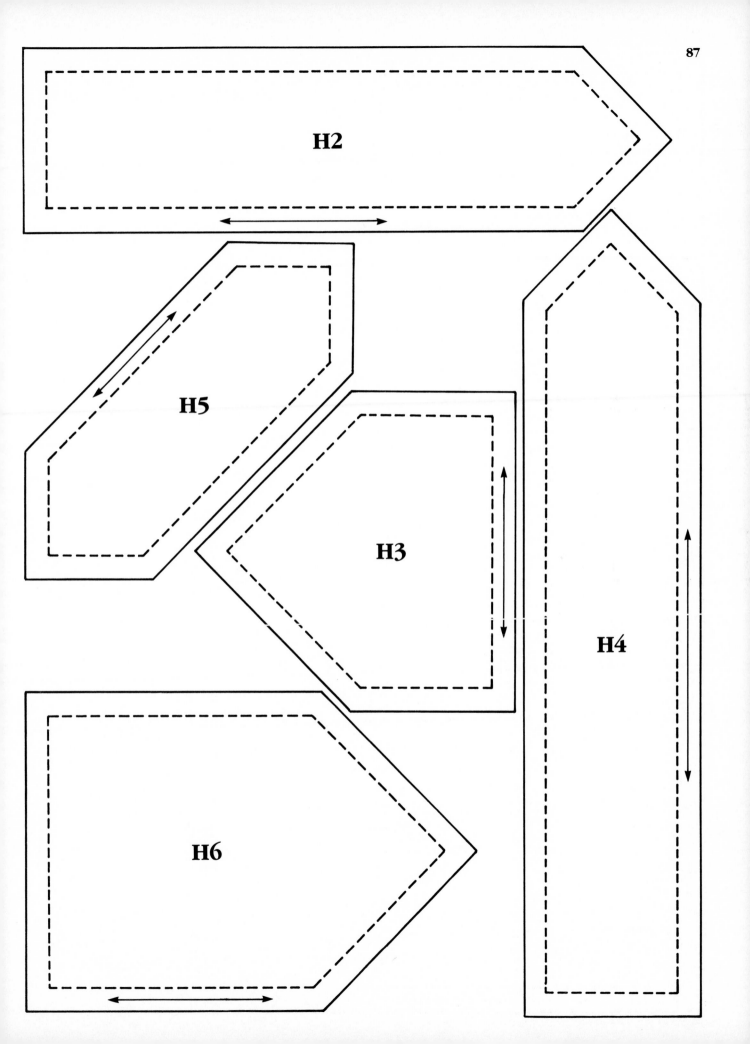

H2

H5

H3

H4

H6

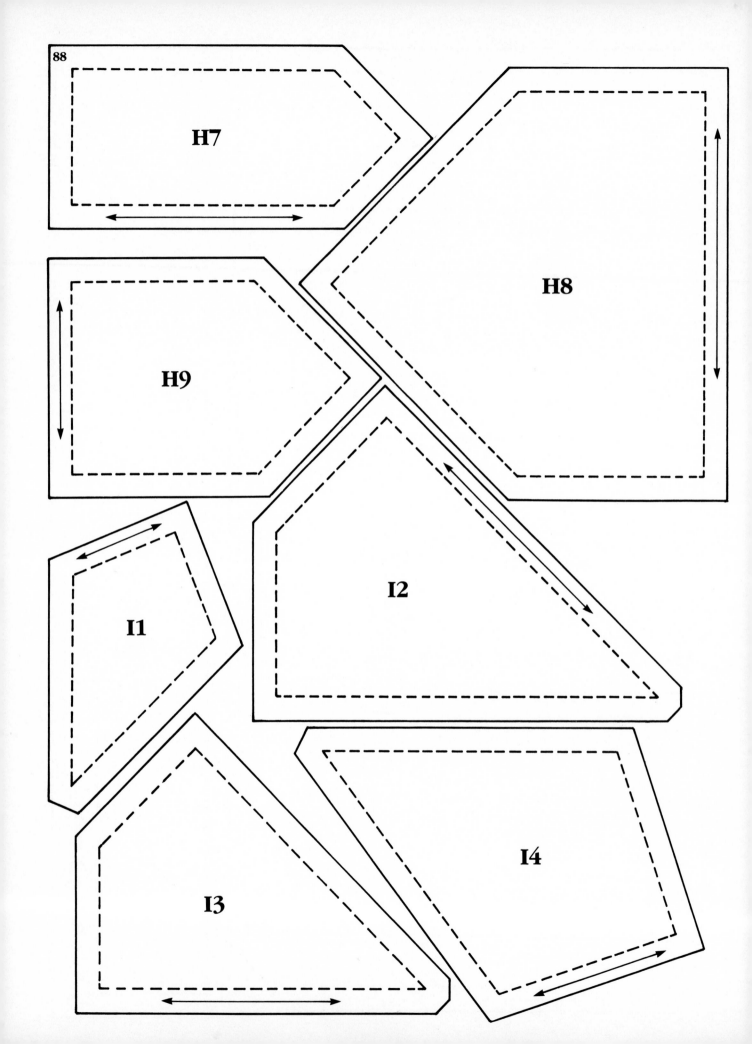

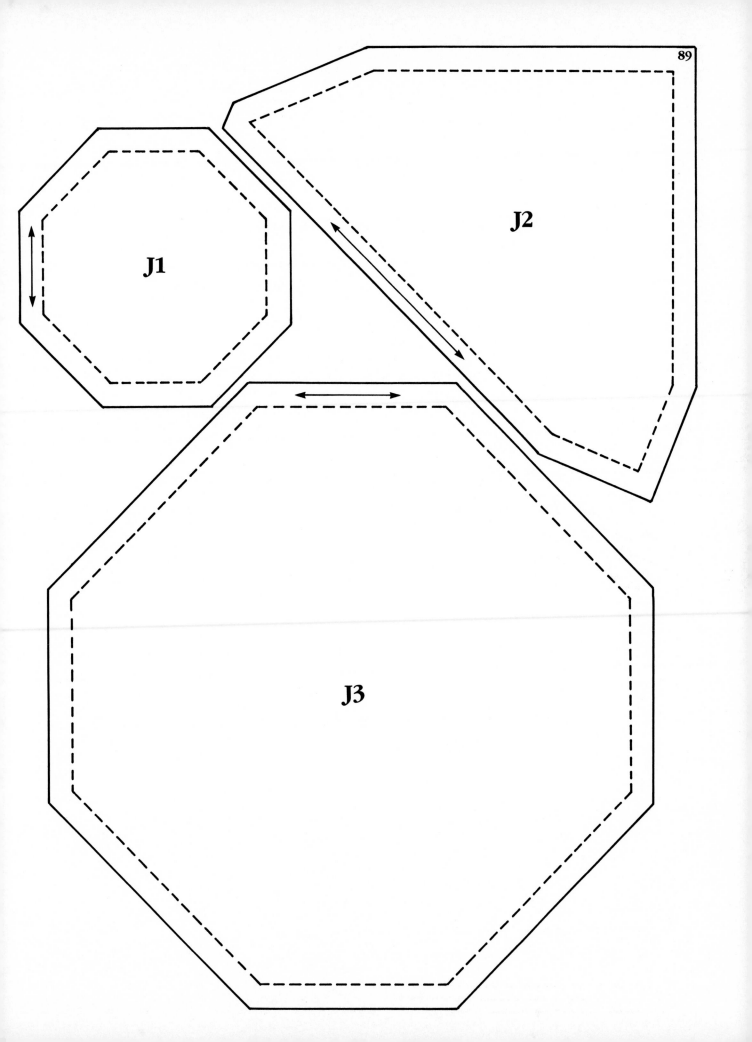

J1

J2

J3

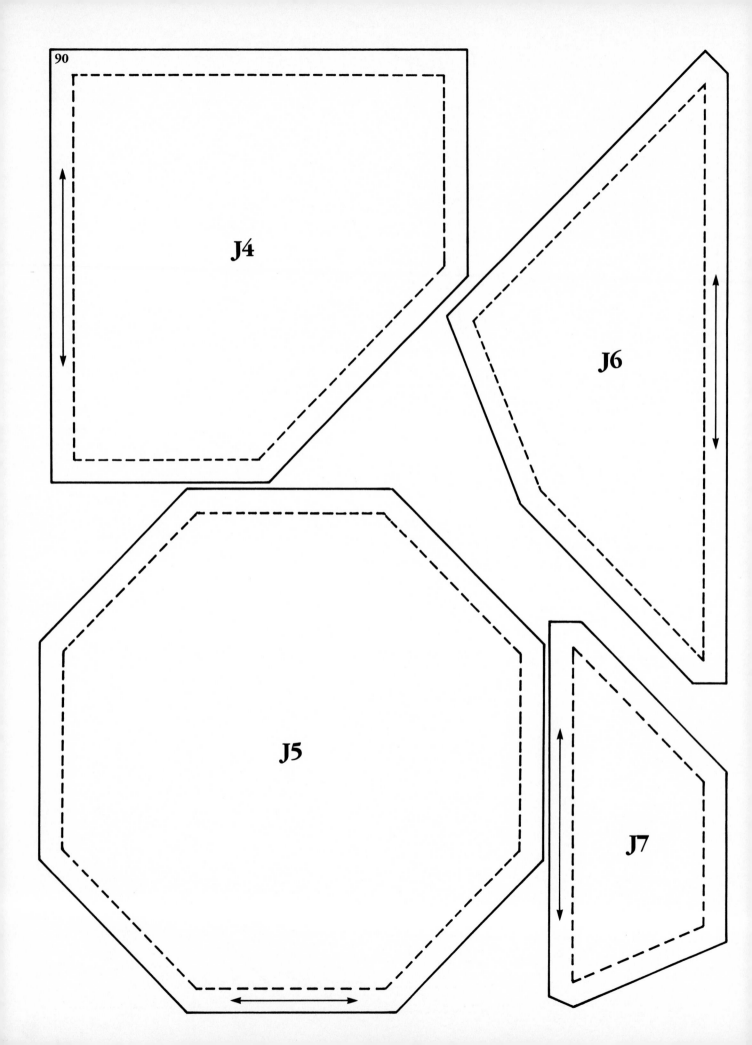

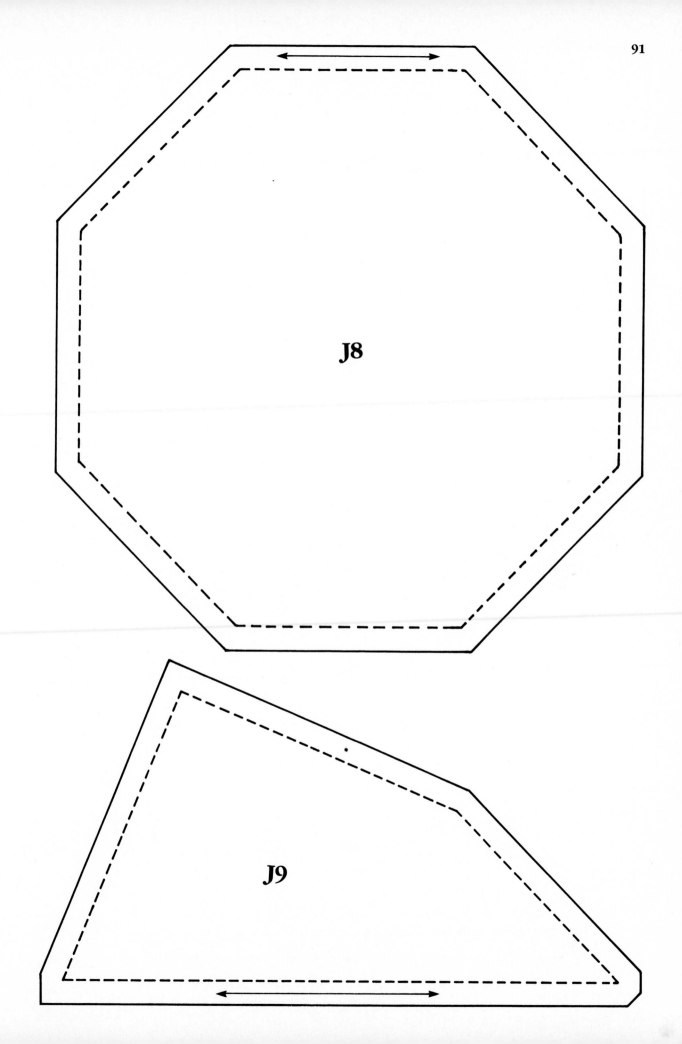

J8

J9

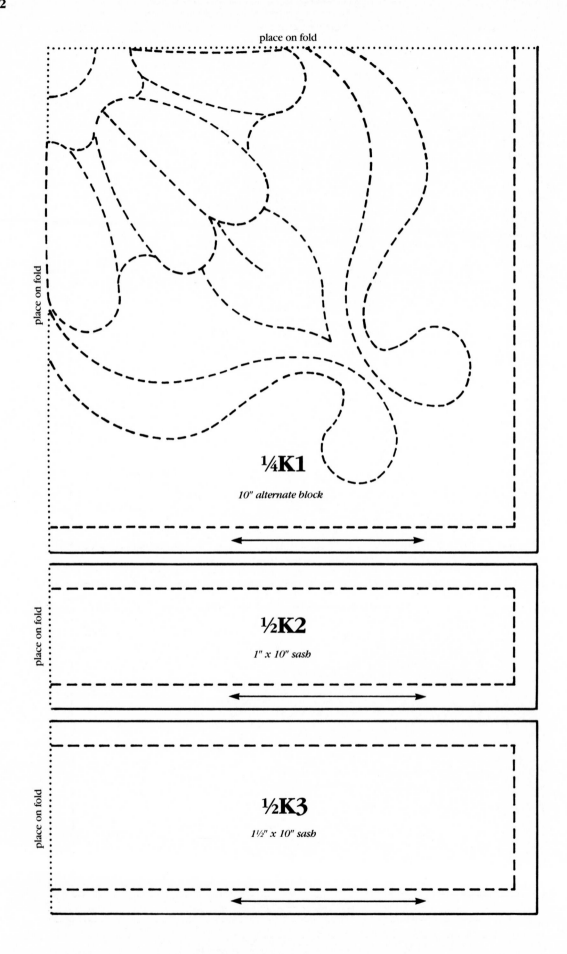

place on fold

place on fold

¼**K1**

10" alternate block

place on fold

½**K2**

1" x 10" sash

place on fold

½**K3**

1½" x 10" sash

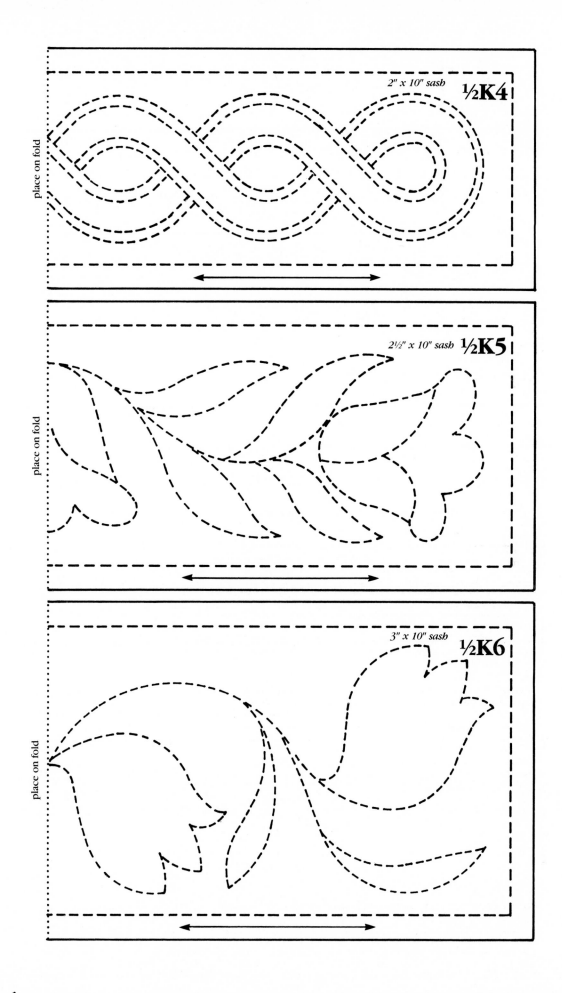

place on fold

2" x 10" sash ½K4

2½" x 10" sash ½K5

3" x 10" sash ½K6

place on fold

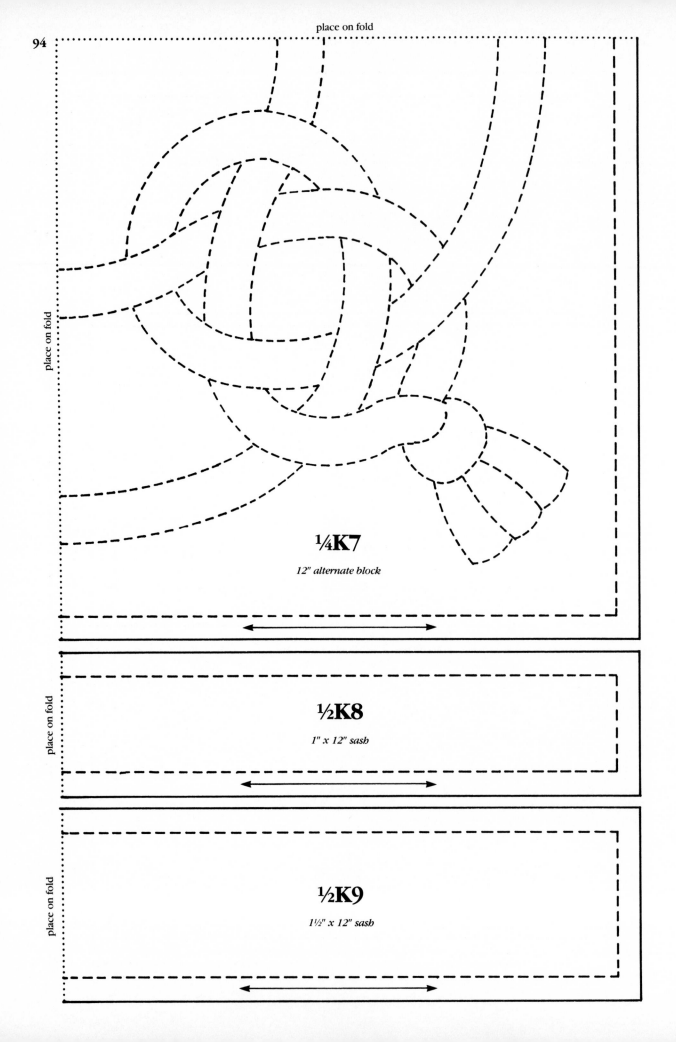

place on fold

¼K7

12" alternate block

½K8

1" x 12" sash

place on fold

½K9

1½" x 12" sash

place on fold

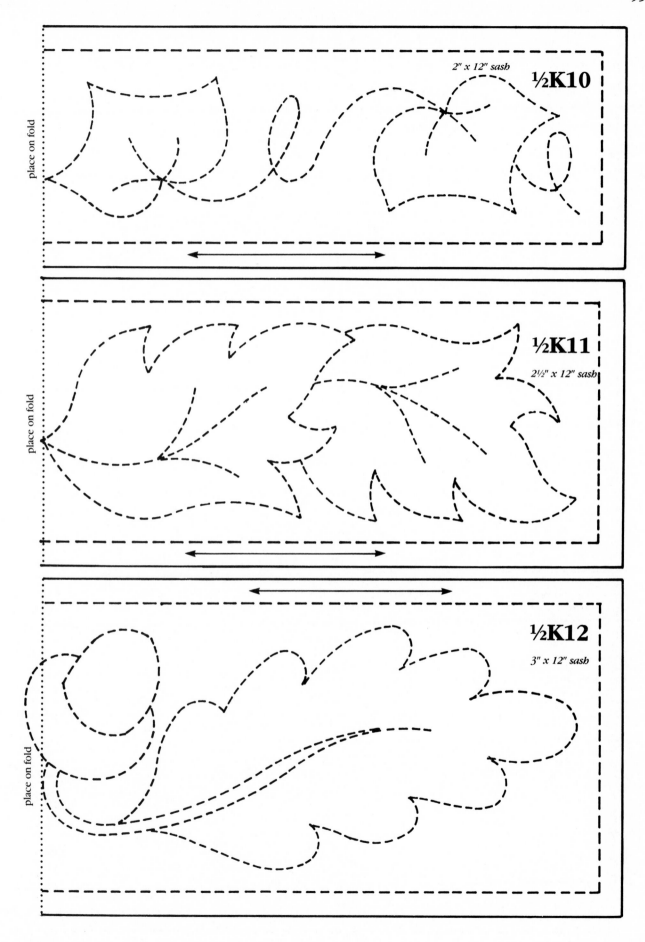

½**K10**

2" x 12" sash

place on fold

½**K11**

2½" x 12" sash

place on fold

½**K12**

3" x 12" sash

place on fold

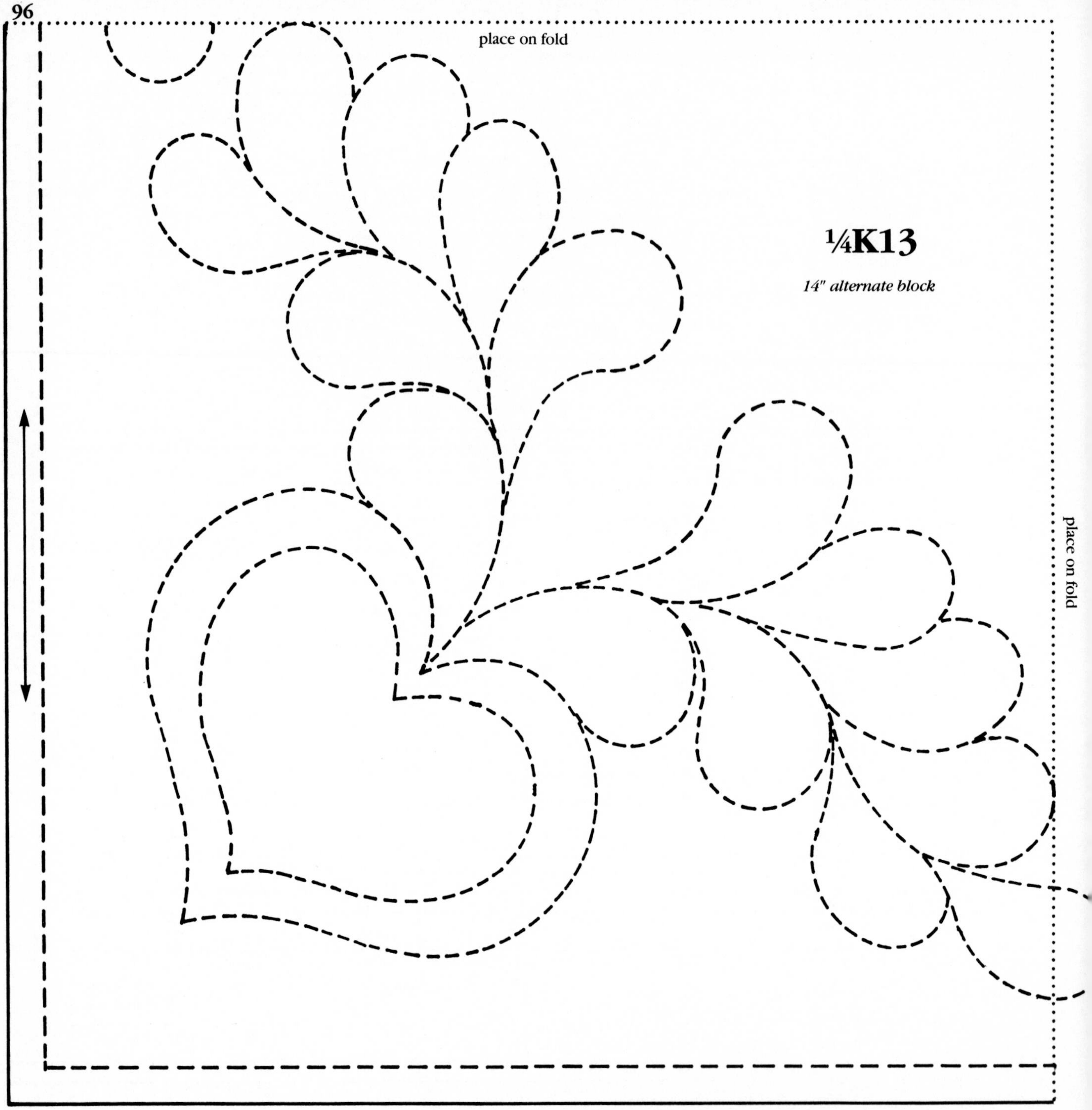

place on fold

¼K13

14" alternate block

place on fold

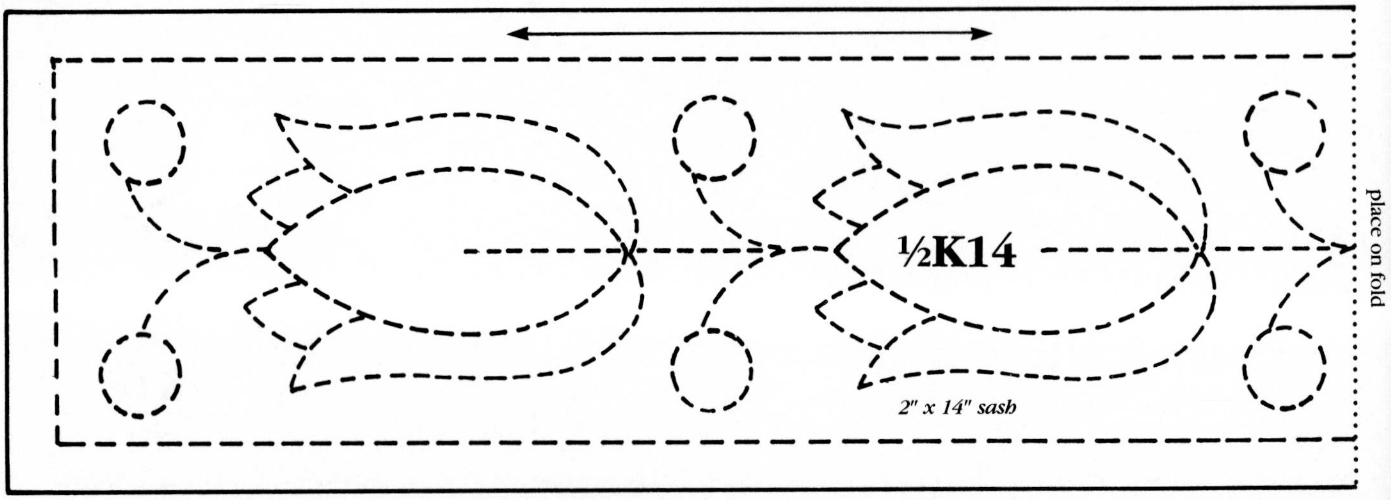

place on fold

½K14

2" x 14" sash

place on fold

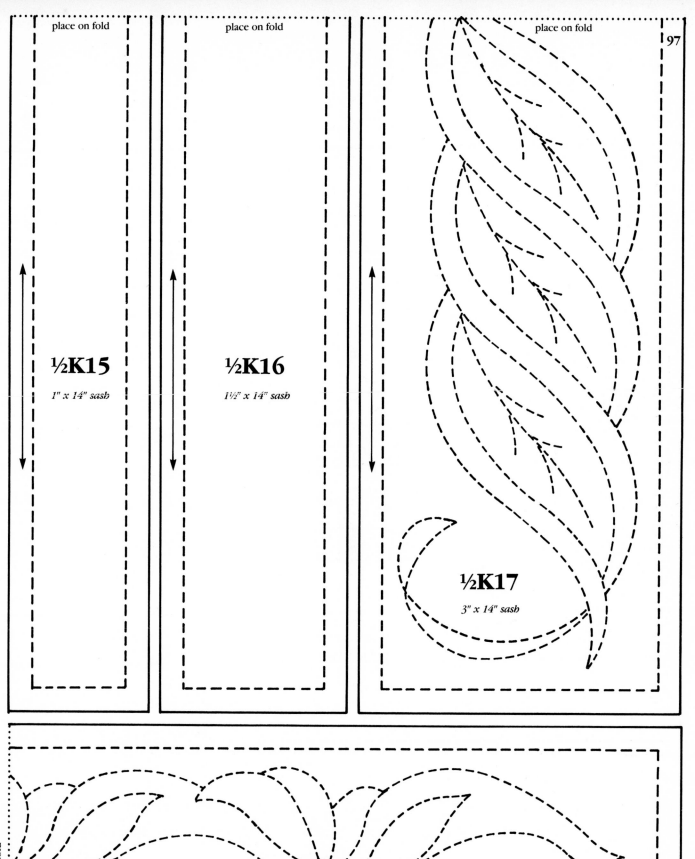

place on fold

½K15

1" x 14" sash

place on fold

½K16

1½" x 14" sash

place on fold

½K17

3" x 14" sash

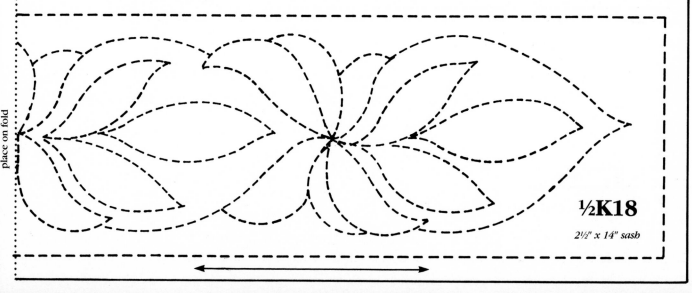

place on fold

½K18

2½" x 14" sash

ABOUT THE AUTHOR

Judy Martin is a freelance author who has been making quilts since 1969. For almost eight years she was senior editor for *Quilter's Newsletter Magazine* and *Quiltmaker,* where her designs and articles were featured regularly. This is her seventh quilting book. Other books by Judy include *Log Cabin Quilts* and *Taking the Math Out of Making Patchwork Quilts* (both co-authored with Bonnie Leman), plus *Patchworkbook, Scrap Quilts, The Rainbow Collection,* and *Shining Star Quilts: Lone Star Variations.* She is currently working on a children's bedtime book and Volume Two of *Judy Martin's Ultimate Book of Quilt Block Patterns.* Judy lives in Wheat Ridge, Colorado, with her husband, Steve. Together, they run Crosley-Griffith Publishing Company. In her spare time, Judy enjoys gardening and, of course, quiltmaking.